Discipline & Spiritual Growth

Leader's Guide

Dixie Ruth Crase
Arthur H. Criscoe

LifeWay Press
Nashville, Tennessee

Reprinted 1998

ISBN 0-8054-9784-6

Parenting by Grace: Discipline & Spiritual Growth Parent's Guide is the text for course CG-0209 in the subject area Home/Family in the Christian Growth Study Plan.

Dewey Decimal Classification Number: 649
Subject Heading: PARENT AND CHILD \ CHILDREN—MANAGEMENT—STUDY AND TEACHING

Printed in the United States of America

LifeWay Press
127 Ninth Avenue, North
Nashville, Tennessee 37234

Contents

The Writers

Dixie Ruth Crase compiled the content material for *Parenting by Grace: Discipline and Spiritual Growth Leader's Guide.* A native of New Mexico, Dr. Crase is a professor of child development at the University of Memphis, Tennessee. She holds degrees from Eastern New Mexico University, Kansas State University, and Ohio State University.

Dr. Crase is a wife, mother, grandmother, professor of early-childhood education, Christian, and director of the Baby Department at Second Baptist Church, Memphis—characteristics that highly qualified her to compile the content for *Parenting by Grace: Discipline and Spiritual Growth.*

Arthur H. Criscoe wrote the teaching procedures and administrative guide for *Parenting by Grace: Discipline and Spiritual Growth Leader's Guide.* A native of Alabama, Dr. Criscoe is the director of the Youth/Children/Preschool Department, Discipleship and Family Development Division, the Sunday School Board, Nashville, Tennessee. He holds degrees from Samford University, Southwestern Baptist Theological Seminary, and Cumberland University. He has done additional study at Texas Christian University, the Catholic University of America, the University of South Carolina, Governors State University, and George Washington University.

Dr. Criscoe has written several books, interactive study guides for videos, and teaching workbooks for Baptist doctrine studies.

With this background Dr. Criscoe was well qualified to write the material for teaching *Parenting by Grace: Discipline and Spiritual Growth.*

Administrative Guide

Welcome to the study of *Parenting by Grace: Discipline and Spiritual Growth.* When you agreed to lead this study, you accepted an important assignment.

The purpose of this *Leader's Guide* is to provide you, the leader, with background information and suggestions that will help you plan a study of *Parenting by Grace: Discipline and Spiritual Growth* in your church. This guide also gives you detailed, step-by-step suggestions and teaching plans for leading this course.

An Overview of *Parenting by Grace: Discipline and Spiritual Growth*

Course Description

Parenting by Grace: Discipline and Spiritual Growth is a parenting course designed to strengthen and enrich families. It provides an opportunity to understand how God's grace applies to parenting and how it can meet particular parenting needs.

This course consists of an introductory session, followed by 10 sessions. The sessions are divided into 5 units of study:

Unit 1: Grace: God's Gift to Parents and Children
- Session 1: Love and Affirmation
- Session 2: Discipline and Guidance

Unit 2: Helping Children Grow According to God's Plan
- Session 3: Physical, Moral, and Spiritual Development
- Session 4: Discipline Grows Children in the Way They Should Go

Unit 3: How to Discipline by Grace
- Session 5: Discipline Affirms Appropriate Behavior
- Session 6: Discipline Finds Alternatives to Replace Inappropriate Behavior

Unit 4: Applying Grace to Your Parenting
- Session 7: Seizing the Teachable Moment
- Session 8: Teaching Through Example

Unit 5: Sustaining Grace in Your Parenting
- Session 9: Experiencing and Celebrating Family
- Session 10: Parents: Sharing and Supporting

Parenting by Grace: Discipline and Spiritual Growth is a part of the Lay Institute for Equipping (LIFE). LIFE is an advanced approach for equipping laypersons for discipleship, leadership, and ministry. LIFE is an educational system that enables Christians to grow at their own pace and to develop skills for ministry according to their spiritual gifts and life goals (see diagram, p. 6).

Elements in LIFE include:
- Daily time with an interactive workbook
- Weekly meetings with a small group
- Application to life experiences

For more information on LIFE courses, contact the Adult Discipleship and Family Department; the Sunday School Board; 127 Ninth Avenue, North; Nashville, TN 37234.

Purpose and Outcomes

The purpose of *Parenting by Grace: Discipline and Spiritual Growth* is to help adults become better parents. The course is designed to help parents understand and utilize God's gift of grace as they love, affirm, discipline, and guide their children to mature, responsible Christian living.

Listed below are some of the primary outcomes from studying this course, identified by the group sessions in which they will be emphasized.

- Parents will better understand the roles of love and affirmation in the parenting process (session 1).
- Parents will better understand the nature and use of discipline in the parenting process (sessions 2, 4, 5, 6).
- Parents will better understand the growth and development of their children (session 3).
- Parents will better understand the teachable moment and how to use it in parenting (session 7).
- Parents will better understand the importance and role of modeling in the parenting process (session 8).
- Parents will better understand how to plan for a regular family time together (session 9).
- Parents will better understand the importance and value of parents' sharing with and supporting one another (session 10).
- Parents will be able to practice the basic principles and guidelines supporting the above concepts and topics (all sessions).

Benefits

After reading the purpose and outcomes of *Parenting by Grace: Discipline and Spiritual Growth,* you can easily see the benefits of this course. There are many ways of looking at these benefits.

Parenting by Grace: Discipline and Spiritual Growth will help parents in all the ways listed in "Purpose and Outcomes." It will help draw families closer together.

Children will benefit in many ways. They will grow to mature, responsible Christian adulthood. The home atmosphere of affirmation and encouragement will help them grow and find God's purpose for their lives. They will have a good foundation for establishing homes of their own in which parenting by grace is practiced.

Churches will benefit as parents learn to share with and support one another. Informal parent-support groups can result from the course. The concepts of parenting by grace can spread throughout the families in a church. Parents who have completed the course become the best promoters to encourage other parents to take the course.

The community will benefit from *Parenting by Grace: Discipline and Spiritual Growth* as stronger homes are established. Children talk with other children at school and other places. Parents talk with other parents in the workplace. The cultures of the world intersect almost daily at the local supermarket, laundromat, and service station. Christian families who practice parenting by grace have the strategic opportunity to model the concepts and principles for the community at large.

DISCIPLE'S CROSS

All Ministries
Experiencing God
MasterLife
The Mind of Christ

Ministry of Worship/Intercession
Disciple's Prayer Life

Ministry of Service
WiseCounsel

Ministry of Evangelism
Witnessing Through Your Relationships
DecisionTime

Ministry of Nurture
Parenting by Grace
Covenant Marriage
Grandparenting by Grace

Ministry of Teaching/Preaching
MasterDesign
BibleGuide
Step by Step Through the Old Testament
Step by Step Through the New Testament

The nation and the world can benefit as parenting-by-grace families in our mobile society move to various parts of the country and world. *Parenting by Grace: Discipline and Spiritual Growth* helps parents function more effectively as salt and light in a decaying and darkening world.

You will benefit personally in many ways as you lead this course. Your own life will be strengthened as you study the concepts of parenting by grace. Your home and family will be strengthened as you practice these concepts. Your skills as a facilitator and group leader will be developed and enhanced as you lead and facilitate the small group through the course. You will have the satisfaction of knowing you have had a part in strengthening the parenting skills of other parents.

How This Course Can Meet Parents' Needs

Parenting by Grace: Discipline and Spiritual Growth seeks to equip Christian parents to be the best they can be. In what areas do parents today need to gain skills and support?

Personal and spiritual needs. *Parenting by Grace: Discipline and Spiritual Growth* can help meet parents' personal and spiritual needs in the following areas.

1. Parents need to recognize the Bible as their trustworthy guide for spiritual growth. By growing spiritually, Christian parents can model a vibrant faith for their children.
2. Parents need to develop Bible-study skills. Effective study of the Scriptures will help them communicate their faith (Deut. 6:6-7) and learn the art of Christian discipline (Prov. 3:12; Eph. 6:4; Heb. 12:7-8).
3. Parents need the supportive fellowship of the church. As ideas and values are discussed from a Christian perspective, parents can often gain new insights on Christian parenting from the church community. "Where two or three are gathered together in my name, there am I in the midst of them" (Matt. 18:20) is a meaningful statement from Jesus to parents in a church, especially those involved in a parent-support group.
4. Parents need to understand religious issues in parenting. The conversion experience and finding God's will in choosing a career are two examples of important steps in a child's life in which effective parenting can make a significant contribution. Parents also have the opportunity to model spiritual values (Deut. 6:6-9; Acts 16:32-34; 2 Tim. 1:5).
5. Parents need to be able to interpret and apply the Bible in practical and relevant ways. The Bible reports the situations in which many families lived, but it does not address many problems of contemporary families. Therefore, parents need to develop skills in applying biblical principles to present-day family situations.
6. Parents need to develop Christian values from which to parent. Values provide the background from which child-rearing decisions are made. Non-Christian as well as Christian values are transmitted to children as they interact with their parents.
7. Parents need to understand the strengths and weaknesses in their own personalities. They especially need to be aware of negative feelings, such as anger and fear, so that they will be better equipped to help their children handle such feelings.
8. Parents need to develop positive self-images. The best parenting is done by parents who genuinely like themselves. When parents do not feel good about themselves, not only are they unhappy and frustrated, but they also provide their children a powerful tool for manipulation.
9. Parents need to understand stages of parenting. These stages are best understood in terms of the developmental needs of the child. As the child grows and matures, different sets of parental skills are needed so that the child gradually becomes less and less dependent on the parents.
10. Parents need to provide appropriate role models for their children, especially in the area of sexual identity. Attitudes about what is appropriate for a male or a female develop in the home. If parents model traditional roles of maleness and femaleness, their children will likely do the same. If the roles are merged to everyone's satisfaction in the family, sons will probably feel comfortable doing household chores, and daughters will not object to doing more traditionally male chores.
11. Parents need to develop interests of their own that are unrelated to parenting. Recognizing that the best parents take time out from parenting, Christian parents should develop a life beyond parenting. Refusing to get away from parenting can lead to fatigue and burnout and can thwart the child's growth toward independence.
12. Parents need to learn how to let go of their children.

Family needs. This course can equip parents to

relate more effectively to other family members.

1. Parents need to understand the role of the Christian family.
2. Parents need to develop an ongoing plan for family worship and Bible study in the home.
3. Parents need to work to enrich their marriages. The best parents have stable, happy marriages.
4. Parents need help in guiding the moral, spiritual, physical, intellectual, social, and emotional development of their children.
5. Parents need to understand how a Christian family lifestyle relates to a secular society.

Special needs. *Parenting by Grace: Discipline and Spiritual Growth* will help parents with the following special needs.

1. Parents need to understand unusual parenting situations in which they find themselves. Such situations may include a homosexual child, a pregnant teenage daughter, a live-in grandchild, criminal activity, abusive behavior, substance abuse, and other issues.
2. Parents need help in managing the unique challenges and rewards of parenting a physically, intellectually, and/or emotionally handicapped child.
3. Parents need help in managing the unique opportunities and hazards of parenting a gifted child.

Sharing needs with other parents. *Parenting by Grace: Discipline and Spiritual Growth* provides a Christian arena in which needs can be acknowledged and parents can provide support and encouragement for one another. Most adults know the delight of sharing good news with a good friend. Most have experienced relief by opening up or admitting what bothers them. Joy is enhanced by sharing, while grief is diminished by sharing. Biblical verses encourage us to bear one another's burden. At the same time, some parents may have been hurt or disillusioned when information or feelings shared were misunderstood or misused. These persons may feel vulnerable when they try to be honest and open with others.

Admittedly, sharing and caring are risky. Ideas and feelings are not always understood or appreciated. However, a much greater risk lies in choosing to live in a restrictive cocoon that allows few persons to come close or be touched by our lives. An openness to life seems essential for developing healthy relationships. Sharing parental needs, concerns, and questions in a supportive group offers an effective approach to becoming a better parent.

Grace: The Foundation of Parenting

Grace is the free, unconditional gift of love and mercy from God (2 Tim. 1:9). It does not depend on anything people may try to do to deserve it. Rather, God has chosen to give His love and mercy to those who accept Jesus Christ, with no strings attached.

Some family members grow up and never know this kind of unconditional love from others in the family. Husbands and wives, parents and children, and brothers and sisters may give and receive love only if certain conditions are met. Such requirements can be heard in comments like "If you'll do this, then I'll love you" or "If you don't stop doing that, I won't love you." Children may never experience love freely given by parents or brothers and sisters. Spouses may live under the constant pressure of having to earn the love of their mates. God's love, however, is freely given, regardless of whether people earn or deserve it.

The biblical concept of grace. God's grace is illustrated in the Old Testament by His continual actions of redemption for His people (Isa. 43:1-15). He reminded them of His watchcare over them and His choice of them as His people. The dearest expression of God's grace was in Jesus Christ. Jesus taught us that God is like a father (Mark 14:36). Even when His children stray like the prodigal son (Luke 15:11-32), God welcomes them back into the family by grace.

The concept of parenting by grace is rooted in the example of God the Father and Jesus the Son (Mark 14:36). But it is also seen in the relationship of God the Father with men and women, the crown of creation (Ps. 8).

God called the ancient Israelites to be His obedient servants and to share Him with other nations. When God set aside the Israelites as His chosen people, He established a covenant relationship that covered every area of their lives, including family relationships.

All of life was covered by the covenant between God and His people. A child born into an Israelite family was part of the whole covenant community. Jewish parents did not discipline their children so that they could enter the covenant community. They disciplined so that their children would live like children already under the covenant and thus continue to be accepted and nurtured through the covenant community.

The Israelites experienced God's grace over and over again. Perhaps the most notable time occurred when God delivered them from bondage in Egypt. God instructed Moses, " 'Come now, and I will send you to Pharaoh, so that you may bring My people, the sons of Israel, out of Egypt' " (Ex. 3:10, NASB). Again God showed His promise of freedom when He told Moses, " 'Say, therefore, to the sons of Israel, "I am the Lord, and I will bring you out from under the burdens of the Egyptians, and I will deliver you from their bondage. ... Then I will take you for My people, and I will be your God; and you shall know that I am the Lord your God, who brought you out from under the burdens of the Egyptians" ' " (Ex. 6:6-7, NASB). The memory of deliverance from Egypt was both a humbling and an encouraging experience. The Israelites were reminded that they had been chosen by sheer grace.

The clearest example of God's grace is seen in what God the Father did when He came as Jesus the Son. Through His gift of grace in Jesus Christ, God has provided the opportunity for redemption and forgiveness for all persons. Paul wrote, "In Him we have redemption through His blood, the forgiveness of our trespasses, according to the riches of His grace" (Eph. 1:7, NASB). Paul also made it clear that neither works nor following the law could earn salvation: "We maintain that a man is justified by faith apart from works of the Law" (Rom. 3:28, NASB).

Salvation is available because God has chosen to give His love freely. This truth is stated beautifully in Ephesians 2:8-9: "By grace you have been saved through faith; and that not of yourselves, it is the gift of God; not as a result of works, that no one should boast" (NASB). Thus, only by accepting God's gift of grace through Jesus Christ can a right relationship with God be entered (Rom. 3:24). This is the foundation for parenting by grace.

Such a relationship is necessary for parents to accomplish their God-given task. Some parents seem to have a knack for parenting, either because their parents were good examples or because they developed their own parenting skills. However, God's gift of grace is available to everyone who believes in Him—including parents. This free gift of grace enables parents and other saved persons to "draw near with confidence to the throne of grace [in prayer]" (Heb. 4:16, NASB). There they can receive forgiveness for their mistakes and can continue in their parenting tasks with the calm assurance that God is with them.

Parenting by grace allows children to know God by seeing Him in their parents. In Jewish homes of the Old Testament, parenting so that their children could come to know God in an intimate relationship was a part of the loyalty and faithfulness God required. This is still true for parents today.

In human relationships grace is seen in the way persons interact with one another. God ordained the family—that is, He placed humans in family relationships so that they could be nurtured, affirmed, disciplined, and guided in an intimate and loving manner. When parents and children are in a right relationship with God, their behavior will be guided by the Holy Spirit (Gal. 5:16-18). As each family member demonstrates the fruit of the Spirit (Gal. 5:22-23) in his interactions in the home, he also demonstrates that God's Spirit lives and works in him.

Parenting by grace requires that Christian parents relate to their children in all circumstances with unconditional love and mercy, as God the Father does. This means to love, affirm, discipline, and guide their children to mature, responsible Christian living. Biblical principles supporting this approach to parenting are:

- God's grace is freely extended to all persons, including parents (2 Tim. 1:9-11).
- Children are gifts from God, and this truth is cause for celebration (Ps. 127:3-5).
- Biblical principles can be applied to life in our world (John 14:23).
- Christian faith can be communicated to children more effectively when parents know what they believe (1 Pet. 3:15).
- Parents grow spiritually when they understand that parenting is a ministry and when they improve their parenting skills (Deut. 6:4-9).
- God's love and grace extend to parents and children in all kinds of families (Rom. 3:23-24; 5:8-11).
- Parenting skills are learned from our parents and therefore are passed from generation to generation (2 Tim. 1:5).
- Parents from all ethnic and cultural backgrounds can maintain their cultural identities as they implement principles of parenting by grace (Acts 10:34-35).

An example of parenting by grace. God provided a model that bridges the Old and New Testament views of rearing children in His choice of Mary and Joseph as Jesus' earthly parents.

When Luke described the events surrounding the unique miracle of Jesus' conception (Luke 1:26-38), he referred to Mary and Joseph as Jesus' parents (Luke 2:43,48). Jesus recognized His own unique Sonship to God (Luke 2:49), but He responded to Mary and Joseph as earthly parents (Luke 2:51).

Mary and Joseph were present at Jesus' birth, and both are mentioned in the incident at the temple when Jesus was 12. Because Joseph was missing at the cross, it has been suggested that he died sometime during the period after the temple incident. However, Jesus had a male model in the home at least during His early childhood.

Luke gave us the only scene from the childhood of Jesus between His birth and the beginning of His earthly ministry (Luke 2:40-52). When Mary and Joseph went looking for Jesus, who had remained behind at the temple, they disciplined Him from love and concern for Him. They recognized His growing independence and spoke to Him from their anxiety, not from hostility for His insensitivity to their feelings. Responding to that concern, Jesus went home with them to Nazareth and continued to be obedient to them. The parenting style of Mary and Joseph can be inferred from this brief incident:

- Mary and Joseph took responsibility for guiding their son.
- They reacted from respect, not hostility.
- Jesus accepted parental authority.
- Mary and Joseph demonstrated parenting by grace.

All biblical teachings on parenting must be interpreted in light of two highly significant factors demonstrating the teachings and modeling of Mary and Joseph's parenting style. These two factors must not be lost in a theology of Christian parenting.

1. Mary and Joseph's calling was to a much higher plane of parenting than required by the law. God called them to their unique role in His plan for sending a Messiah (Matt. 1:18-25; Luke 1:26-28). God also calls Christian parents today to an equally profound task so that His divine will for families can be accomplished and His mission for the world can be realized.
2. Mary and Joseph provided the earthly parenting for God's only Son. Jesus did not spring full grown to earth. Rather, God chose for Him to grow through the normal processes of human growth. God entrusted His earthly parents with providing the love, affirmation, discipline, and guidance He needed to grow as God willed: "The Child continued to grow and become strong, increasing in wisdom; and the grace of God was upon Him" (Luke 2:40, NASB). And the grace of God was on Him! Who were the earthly ministers of that grace of God being poured on the boy Jesus? None other than Mary and Joseph!

"Jesus kept increasing in wisdom and stature, and in favor with God and men" (Luke 2:52, NASB). This one verse spells out the task of Christian parenting. No other verse in the Gospel describes the growth of the child Jesus so completely. The four areas of growth—wisdom (mental and emotional growth), stature (physical growth), in favor with God (spiritual growth) and man (growth in personal relationships)—can be viewed as covering the entire scope of individual growth.

The elements of Christian parenting—love and affirmation, discipline and guidance—serve to help modern children grow in wisdom and stature and in favor with God and significant persons. This is parenting by grace.

Experiencing *Parenting by Grace: Discipline and Spiritual Growth*

Target Audience

Parenting by Grace: Discipline and Spiritual Growth is for adults who have children ranging in age from infants through adolescents. Although it is desirable for both parents to take the course together, it is not required. The course is also ideal for single parents and parents of blended families.

Several assumptions were made about the target group as this course was developed. Some of these assumptions were drawn from the work in adult learning by Malcolm Knowles.

The parent is a Christian. The course is built on the biblical concept of grace and the model of God's loving, forgiving, and disciplining us. The terminology and activities presuppose that the parent is a Christian. However, the course should not be restricted to Christian parents. Some parents who are not Christians may wish to take the course. They should be welcomed. Their involvement in the course could be a special time when God works in them about the need to become Christian parents.

If you have non-Christian parents in the group, be aware of and sensitive to this fact. At times you may need to give a more complete explanation of a biblical concept or Scripture reference. Pray privately for these parents. At times a follow-up visit in the home and a verbal witness would be appropriate.

The parent can read and write. The materials are written on an eighth-grade reading level and call for written involvement. Of course, parents who cannot read or write should not be excluded from the course. You need to be aware of the special needs of nonreaders who enroll. It would be ideal for the spouse of a nonreader to take the course at the same time so that the two can work together.

The parent can devote several hours each week to the course. The course is intensive, calling for a high degree of involvement both in individual study and in practicing the concepts and guidelines with children. If work schedules or other factors do not allow a parent adequate time, it would be better for that parent to postpone taking the course until an appropriate time schedule can be worked out. Simply to read the lessons and attend the group sessions would short-circuit the learning process. It is imperative that the parents complete the learning activities in the *Parent's Guide* and complete the assignments for "on-the-job" experience with their children.

Parents come from various ethnic and cultural backgrounds. Other than using the English language, the course is not restricted to persons of any ethnic or cultural background. Parents from all ethnic and cultural backgrounds will want to maintain their unique characteristics as they practice the concepts and principles of parenting by grace. Parents learn and grow from sharing with other parents their backgrounds and experiences.

Parents see themselves as responsible adult learners capable of self-direction. This assumption has significant implications for *Parenting by Grace: Discipline and Spiritual Growth.* You as facilitator will want to work to create a climate of openness, freedom, and respect during the course. The parents themselves should be involved in planning, carrying out, and evaluating their learning experiences. You will want to be flexible as you plan and lead the course. For example, the learning goals suggested for each lesson may need to be adjusted, depending on the needs of the parents in your group.

Parents bring all of their experiences with them to the course. Because of this assumption, the key teaching method throughout the group sessions is discussion. Parents learn from sharing with other parents. Their experiences represent a vast reservoir of learning potential. This reservoir can be used as you help guide the discussions.

Parents are problem-centered in their learning. The education of children and youth often uses the banking concept of learning, that is, the accumulation of knowledge for use in the future. Not so with adult learners. They are focused on the here and now, ready for help with problems they already face. This assumption does not mean that the approach to learning in *Parenting by Grace: Discipline and Spiritual Growth* is negative. It means that a high degree of motivation is already present. The course makes extensive use of case studies, giving parents the opportunity to "hang" their problems on someone else and view them more objectively. Many teachable moments will surface throughout the course when the concepts being learned fit a problem or a need the parent is experiencing.

Parents want to develop their parenting skills. *Parenting by Grace: Discipline and Spiritual Growth* offers an unparalleled opportunity for adults to grow and develop as Christian parents. The more Christlike our lives become, the closer we can follow the model of parenting by grace. Without this intrinsic motivation to improve, the course will not be effective. The fact that a parent enrolls in the course is a good indication that this motivation is already present.

Course Model

Parenting by Grace: Discipline and Spiritual Growth has three elements in its design. These elements interlock, and each one is essential. All three parts must be present throughout the course.

Individual study. The *Parent's Guide* is designed for a person to work through individually. Each lesson provides input on the concept or principles studied.

On-the-job experience. *Parenting by Grace: Discipline and Spiritual Growth* requires much more than cognitive input. Specific assignments in the *Parent's Guide* ask parents to practice the guidelines and principles. In fact, most learning in this course will take place as parents practice affirmation, encouragement, discipline, and guidance with their children.

Group sessions. The small-group session brings together the individual study and on-the-job experience as parents discuss and reflect on their learning. The group provides a setting in which parents can examine and discuss their experiences in parenting. There they can analyze their experiences objectively and can understand cause-and-effect relationships. They can determine which actions helped or hindered their children. They can compare the effects of their parenting behavior with the intentions of their actions. The small group also helps parents generalize about the next time the same kind of parenting situation occurs. They are able to plan different behavior patterns and to anticipate their action when a similar event occurs. The group is able to draw conclusions helpful to every member.

Design of the *Parent's Guide*

The *Parent's Guide* follows a carefully designed plan that encourages optimal learning. Several distinctive features characterize the *Parent's Guide.*

Self-instructional. The *Parent's Guide* is self-instructional. The guide itself serves as the teacher; it is not necessary for you to prepare and present lectures on the lessons. The parent learns from working through the material. This frees the group session for learning to take place on a higher level and to go beyond what the parent has already learned from working through the lesson.

Interactive. The *Parent's Guide* is interactive. The learner must do more than simply read the material. Activities are included to involve the learner.

A threefold pattern makes the *Parent's Guide* interactive. First, input or information is presented. Second, an activity is called for to involve the learner in some way. These activities are varied in nature, ranging from written exercises to interacting with the child. Third, feedback is usually given to let learners evaluate their response to the activity. Sometimes this feedback is given by interacting with other parents in the group session.

Goal-oriented. The goal of becoming a better parent is constantly kept in view. General and specific learning goals for each lesson help keep the course focused. They also remind learners that they must seek to implement the concepts and guidelines in actual practice with their children. These goals are not to be interpreted as rigid and unchangeable. At times parents may need to adjust the goals to meet their specific needs.

Self-paced. The *Parent's Guide* is designed for learners to work through at their own pace. The only restriction is that each lesson must be completed before the small group meets to discuss that lesson. In most instances one lesson will be covered each week. If a person works through the lesson at the beginning of the week and completes the written activities, then most of the week can be spent actually practicing the concept and principles with the child.

Interdependent. The *Parent's Guide* is interdependent in two ways. First, it is linked with the on-the-job experience and with the small-group sessions. Second, the lessons are interdependent and interlocking. They build on one another.

Format. Each lesson in the *Parent's Guide* follows a prescribed format.

Looking Back
Overview
Learning Goals
Input on the Specific Topic of the Lesson
Checkpoint
Reflection and Application
Summary
Looking Ahead

"Looking Back" is a review of the preceding lesson. This section reinforces learning and ties the two lessons together.

"Overview" is a brief preview of the lesson to be studied. The overview serves as an advance organizer to let the learner know key points to be studied.

"Learning Goals" gives a general or overall learning goal for the lesson and specific outcomes. These goal statements let learners know exactly what they should be able to do after the lesson.

Next input on the specific topic of the lesson is given.

"Checkpoint" is a test that measures achievement of the learning goals. This section comes directly from the learning goals.

"Reflection and Application" is a section of activities that give the parent practice in implementing the concept and guidelines covered in the lesson. Two types of activities are included: (1) questions and exercises the parent uses to reflect on the input of the lesson and (2) exercises and assignments for the parent to do with the child. When a specific learning goal is of such nature that it cannot be measured precisely, an activity related to it is included here rather than in "Checkpoint."

This section also contains reflection-and-application activities based on learning acquired in previous sessions. These activities serve to review and reinforce concepts and guidelines studied earlier.

"Summary" is a concise synopsis of the lesson. This section provides feedback for the parent's work in "Checkpoint." It also reinforces learning by reviewing the lesson.

"Looking Ahead" contains a brief summary of the next lesson and an assignment related to it.

Design of the *Leader's Guide*

The section "Leader's Plans" in this guide is an integral part of the educational design of the course. It provides a suggested step-by-step plan for you to follow as you plan for and lead each session.

Each group session provides specific, measurable learning goals or objectives supporting the broad learning outcomes of the course. These learning goals help you maintain a focus as you guide each session.

The plans for each session also include the sections "Before the Session" and "During the Session." "After the Session" is recommended for each session but is printed only at the end of the introductory session.

You will note as you study the leader's plans that the sessions are experiential in nature, with a high degree of involvement and discussion.

Design of the Group Session

The group session has four parts or steps. Each part has a definite purpose and is linked with the step before it and with the next step.

Debriefing. The debriefing activity includes a brief review of the previous session. It includes a checkup or report on the assignments members completed. Members may also discuss any experiences they had between sessions applying what they learned from a previous session.

Presentation. This step summarizes the lesson being studied. It does not mean that you present this summary; you lead the group in its own summary of the lesson. It is not necessary to present every detail of the lesson. The parent has already worked through the lesson at home. This presentation covers the highlights of the lesson and emphasizes the main points.

Skill development. As the heart of the session, this section focuses on discussion and involvement. It provides the means for transferring knowledge to practical application.

Preview and assignment. This brief step contains two segments: a preview of the next session and a home assignment. At this time you can help members relate this lesson to the total course and understand how the next lesson will move them closer to the overall goal of the course. Completion of the home assignment is essential preparation for the next session.

This model is initiated again as the group meets for the next session. If a group is covering two lessons each time it meets, then the model is worked through twice in one meeting. The model can be diagrammed as shown.

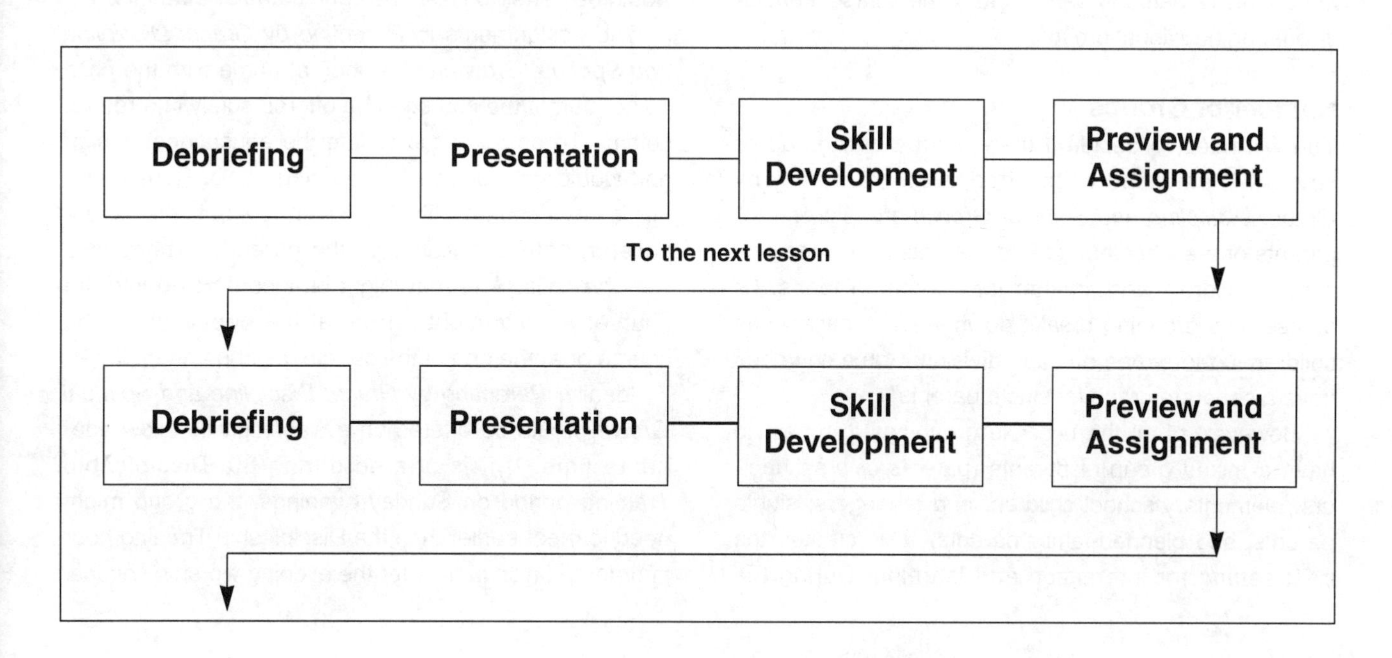

How to Plan for *Parenting by Grace: Discipline and Spiritual Growth*

Planning Responsibility

Many churches have a Discipleship Training council that plans various training courses. Some churches have a leader-training director responsible for administering LIFE. In other churches the Discipleship Training director, pastor, another church-staff member, or another leader has this responsibility.

If your church has a family-enrichment committee, it would be the ideal group to plan *Parenting by Grace: Discipline and Spiritual Growth.* This committee could work closely with the person responsible for the LIFE system and with the Discipleship Training director. The planning committee could divide into subcommittees with specific assignments for various planning responsibilities. Another approach could be to enlist other persons to serve on temporary committees or workgroups.

Group Size

The ideal group size for *Parenting by Grace: Discipline and Spiritual Growth* is between 9 and 12 persons. The course is effective with larger or smaller groups, but you should work to limit the group size to between 9 and 12 persons. This ideal size is small enough for everyone in the large group to share and take part in the discussion. It is also large enough to form at least three small groups with 3 or 4 persons in each group. If more than 12 persons want to study the course, consider offering additional groups.

Number of Groups

You will need to decide if there will be one group or several. Some churches offer three *Parenting by Grace: Discipline and Spiritual Growth* groups: one for parents of preschoolers, one for parents of elementary-school children, and another for parents of teens. Of course, this grouping breaks down when a parent has children in more than one age division. Some churches have a separate group for single parents.

However, of all the possible groupings it is best to have a mixed group of parents (parents of preschoolers, elementary-school children, and teenagers; single parents; and blended-family parents). This creates the best setting for interaction and learning. During the group sessions parents will often be asked to divide into small groups according to the ages of their children.

If your church has several *Parenting by Grace: Discipline and Spiritual Growth* groups meeting concurrently, it would be good to have a banquet at the end of the course involving all of the groups. All family members should be included.

Schedule

Parenting by Grace: Discipline and Spiritual Growth includes 10 sessions and 1 introductory session. Each lesson in the *Parent's Guide* requires a one-hour group session.

The 11-week plan. Some churches conduct *Parenting by Grace: Discipline and Spiritual Growth* for 11 weeks. The first week is the introductory session, and the 10 lessons are covered in subsequent weeks. The intensity of the course and the involvement in outside assignments to be completed between the sessions make this schedule ideal.

The 6-week plan. Some churches may choose to schedule the course for 6 weeks, with two-hour sessions covering two lessons. The introductory lesson would be covered the first week. Groups following this plan should have adequate time to spend on the assignments at home.

Other schedules. Some churches may lengthen this course by spending two weeks on each lesson. This would require 21 or 22 weeks to complete the course. However, to sustain interest and motivation, it would be better to finish the course earlier than this.

The assignments in *Parenting by Grace: Discipline and Spiritual Growth* to be done at home with the child do not permit the course to be offered solely in a retreat setting. To do so would violate the educational design and would not achieve the learning goals. Remember, this is not a course with only cognitive input; it is experiential in nature, building on the parent's experiences with the child. A retreat might be incorporated into the course. An overnight retreat at the beginning of the course or at the end of the course might be an option.

Ideally, *Parenting by Grace: Discipline and Spiritual Growth* would be offered on a weeknight to allow adequate time. If it is offered during the Discipleship Training period on Sunday evenings, the group might need to meet earlier than the Discipleship Training hour in order to finish in time for the evening worship service.

Your church schedule will determine your need to make adjustments. It will be important to have sufficient time to conduct group sessions without being rushed.

When the schedule is set, place the study on the church calendar. Any time of the year is appropriate to offer the course.

Leader and Facilitator

Each group will need a leader or facilitator. It would be ideal for the church to send the facilitator to a national, state, or associational meeting to be trained to lead *Parenting by Grace: Discipline and Spiritual Growth.*

Each group leader/facilitator is a unique individual with unique gifts and leadership capabilities. It would be a mistake to develop a detailed leader profile that every leader must fit. However, some obvious characteristics and qualities are most helpful for leading and facilitating this study effectively:

- Be a growing Christian
- Be a growing parent
- Be an active church member
- Have a teachable spirit
- Have a healthy attitude toward children
- Possess good interpersonal-relationship skills
- Be open in attitude
- Be an energetic self-starter
- Have the ability to facilitate and lead a small group
- Experience beforehand *Parenting by Grace: Discipline and Spiritual Growth*
- Exhibit a willingness to lead and an enthusiasm for *Parenting by Grace: Discipline and Spiritual Growth*
- Be committed to the concepts taught in the course

For information on the group leader's specific responsibilities, see the section "Your Role as Leader and Facilitator," beginning on page 20.

Meeting Place

A large classroom is ideal for the group. Most homes do not have adequate space, especially for the use of visual aids. The meeting place should be large enough to allow members freedom to move about. Small groups are formed numerous times during the course, and the room needs to be able to accommodate them.

Vary the room arrangement from time to time and do not use the same setup for every session. Tables are recommended because they provide a good writing surface and are a natural setting for dividing into small groups.

If you use chairs without tables, position the chairs so that every person can see all other members. Rows are not effective for the type of activities suggested for the sessions. A semicircular arrangement is recommended.

The walls of the room should accommodate teaching posters suggested for use in every session. If masking tape would damage the walls, easels can be used for the posters.

Resources

Two primary resources are needed to conduct this study:

- *Parenting by Grace: Discipline and Spiritual Growth Parent's Guide* (item 7764-06)
- *Parenting by Grace: Discipline and Spiritual Growth Leader's Guide* (item 7201-03)

Each facilitator will need a *Leader's Guide* and a *Parent's Guide.* Each participant will need a copy of the *Parent's Guide.* If a husband and a wife take the course together, each of them needs a copy of the *Parent's Guide.* Activities throughout the *Parent's Guide* require written responses from each learner.

Resources should be ordered from 10 to 12 weeks prior to the first session. Even though shipping normally takes from 4 to 6 weeks from the date the order is received, leaders will need time to prepare for the introductory session.

The church will need to determine how to pay for the resources. Some churches ask the parents to pay for the *Parent's Guide,* while other churches purchase them through the church budget.

Also order a copy of *Home Life, ParentLife,* and *Living with Teenagers* for each participant.

Order materials with the order forms your church receives quarterly; write or call the Customer Service Center; the Sunday School Board; 127 Ninth Avenue, North; Nashville, TN 37234; 1-800-458-2772; or visit your Baptist Book Store or Lifeway Christian Store.

Supplies you will need include a large roll of newsprint or white paper, poster board, a roll of adding-machine tape, felt-tip markers, pencils, a chalkboard, chalk, an eraser, and masking tape. Several translations of the Bible would also be useful.

Child Care

Adequate plans and provisions should be made for child care. Some churches leave this for each parent to arrange, but it would be better if the church provided child care.

Records

The proper record forms should be obtained from the Discipleship Training director.

Recognition

Plans should be made to recognize every person completing the course. The facilitator should receive special recognition.

Some churches have a banquet to recognize those completing the course. Many churches include the parents and their children at this banquet and designate them parenting-by-grace families. Other churches have a special recognition during a worship service at church. *Parenting by Grace: Discipline and Spiritual Growth* diplomas could be presented, and the pastor could preach on the theme of the family and home.

Follow-up

Some persons completing the course form parent-support groups and continue meeting on their own, as recommended in lesson 10. Parent-support groups are informal and unstructured. They meet in parents' homes to discuss problems and opportunities of mutual concern. These groups should be encouraged. They should not be viewed as a threat to any program organization in the church.

Persons completing the course should be made aware of other training opportunities. Consider starting new Discipleship Training groups for these persons, using other LIFE courses or short-term courses.

Promotion and Enlistment

Effective promotion and enlistment are keys to the success of *Parenting by Grace: Discipline and Spiritual Growth* in a church. Promote the course within the church family and outside the church family.

Promotion Within the Church Family

Most churches offer *Parenting by Grace: Discipline and Spiritual Growth* primarily for their own members. Many ways may be used to promote the course within the church.

Pulpit announcements. This method, along with the church newsletter and church bulletin, is the most effective method of promoting the course.

Church Sunday bulletin. Here are two sample blurbs. Change the details to fit your situation.

What?
Parenting by Grace:
Discipline and Spiritual Growth
When?
Sunday, October 7
Where?
Room 710 at the church
Why?
To help us become better parents

PARENTING BY GRACE:
DISCIPLINE AND SPIRITUAL GROWTH
... begins next week. This 11-week course will meet each Thursday, 7:00–8:00 p.m. Enroll today by calling the church office, 282-4002.

Church newsletter. Here are two sample announcements that could be used along with the Parenting by Grace logo. Change the details to meet your needs.

***PARENTING BY GRACE: DISCIPLINE AND SPIRITUAL GROWTH* IS ABOUT . . .**

- Grace: God's gift to parents and children
- How to help children grow according to God's plan
- How to discipline by grace
- How to apply grace to your parenting
- How to sustain grace in your parenting

Make plans now to attend this 11-week course. It will meet in room 710 each Thursday, 7:00–8:00 p.m., beginning October 11. Child care will be provided.

Parenting by Grace: Discipline and Spiritual Growth begins October 11! This 11-week course is designed to help Christian parents understand and exercise the gift of God's grace in parenting. The course will meet each Thursday, 7:00–8:00 p.m., in room 710. Pre-enroll by calling the church office. Child care will be provided.

Letters to parents. Here are two sample letters. Include the Parenting by Grace logo to enhance your letters. Change the copy to meet your needs.

Dear Parent:

The need for strong families has never been greater than today. Moral foundations are crumbling, and strong pressures continually work to pull families apart. Christian parenting has never been more significant.

Parenting by Grace: Discipline and Spiritual Growth is a course that will help us become better parents. It will teach us to apply the concepts and principles of parenting found in the Bible to our homes today.

Parenting by Grace: Discipline and Spiritual Growth will begin October 11 and will meet in room 710 each Thursday, 7:00–8:00 p.m., for 11 weeks. Child care will be provided.

I hope you will be a part of this important study.

Sincerely,

Dear Parent:

How would you like to know more about—
- the role of affirmation in parenting?
- the use of positive discipline in parenting?
- the teachable moment and how to use it?
- the role of modeling in parenting?

Would you like to be able to put these concepts into practice with your child? Then plan to enroll in *Parenting by Grace: Discipline and Spiritual Growth.* The course will meet each Thursday, 7:00–8:00 p.m., for 11 weeks. Call the church (282-4002) to find out more and to pre-enroll. Child care will be provided.

Sincerely,

Posters. Here are two sample posters. Fill in the blanks.

Parenting involves:

- Affirmation
- Teachable moments
- Modeling
- Love
- Grace
- Discipline
- Development
- Guidance
- Encouragement

Attend *Parenting by Grace: Discipline and Spiritual Growth* and learn more.

When :________________________

Where: ________________________

Child care will be provided.

Parenting by Grace:
Discipline and Spiritual Growth

For parents who want to grow in their parenting skills

When: ______________________

Where: ______________________

Child care will be provided.

Word of mouth. This is a very effective means of promotion.

Church organizations. The Church Council could be asked to promote *Parenting by Grace: Discipline and Spiritual Growth* through Sunday School, Discipleship Training, Music Ministry, Woman's Missionary Union, and Brotherhood.

Baby-dedication events. This course could be promoted during these special times and others your church might conduct.

Deacon visitation. Deacons could be enlisted to publicize the course as they visit the families of the church.

Promotion Outside the Church Family

Many churches use *Parenting by Grace: Discipline and Spiritual Growth* to reach and help parents who may not be members of a church. Not only does this provide an important ministry for families, but the church is also able to reach many of them for Christ and for church membership.

Here are some suggestions for promotion to the community at large.

- Leaflets in doctors' offices, barber shops, and beauty salons—anywhere interested parents might visit (use camera-ready copy for church-bulletin insert/flier)
- Radio/television announcements (many of these can be provided as a free public service)
- Newspaper announcements
- Posters in shopping centers
- Letters to prospects
- Special visitation campaign
- Special telephone campaign
- Take-home notes to parents of children in your church's weekday-education program (use camera-ready copy for church-bulletin insert/flier)

COUNTDOWN CALENDAR

Date	Time Before Course Begins	Action	Person(s) Responsible	Completion Date
	6 months	Schedule group(s).		
	6 months	Enlist facilitator(s).		
	6 months	Provide special training for facilitator(s).		
	3 months	Order resources.		
	2 months	Begin promotion-and-awareness campaign; mail first letter.		
	2 months	Make arrangements for child care.		
	6 weeks	Work with facilitator(s) to select meeting place(s).		
	4 weeks	Increase promotion and awareness.		
	3 weeks	Mail second letter.		
	3 weeks	Obtain proper record/enrollment forms.		
	3 weeks	Conduct preregistration.		
	After course is completed	Request Church Study Course diplomas.		
	After course is completed	Conduct special recognition service for persons completing the course.		
	After course is completed	Encourage parent-support groups.		
	After course is completed	Encourage participants to enroll in other training courses.		

Leader's Plans

Your Role as Leader and Facilitator

Leader Preparation

Before you make specific plans to lead and facilitate the sessions, you need to:

- Read the *Parent's Guide* and the leader's plans for all of the sessions, beginning on page 25 in this guide. This advance study will alert you to any long-range plans you need to make.
- Plan for members to earn the *Parenting by Grace: Discipline and Spiritual Growth* Church Study Course Diploma. Requirements for this diploma are in this *Leader's Guide* (p. 80).
- Pray for the Holy Spirit's guidance as you prepare to lead the sessions.

Planning Each Session

After you have done advance planning, plan one session at a time.

- Read and study the appropriate lesson in the *Parent's Guide* as you prepare for each session. Complete the learning activities in the *Parent's Guide.*
- Carefully study the suggested plans in the section "Leader's Plans" in this *Leader's Guide.* Work through the learning activities, worksheets, and case studies in advance to experience what you want participants to experience during the session.
- Spend time thinking about the members of the group. Think of their families and any particular needs they may have. Evaluate the suggested activities in light of your members' needs and circumstances. For example, if no parent in the group has a preschooler, then obviously, you would eliminate the activities related to preschoolers to spend more time on activities related to the ages of the members' children.
- Decide which learning activities to use. *You will not have enough time to use them all.* Plan how you will adapt the suggested activities to fit the needs and interests of the participants as well as your own skills as facilitator.
- Prepare your own teaching plan. Plan how much time you will allow for each activity. You will want to be flexible and sensitive to members' needs and not be rushed in moving through a session. At the same time, you will want to have a tentative time schedule in mind for the session. Here is a suggested schedule for the major parts of each session.

Debriefing	10 minutes
Presentation	10 minutes
Skill Development	35 minutes
Preview and Assignment	5 minutes

- Prepare teaching posters for the session (if required) using newsprint and felt-tip markers of different colors. You may want to enlist other persons to assist you in preparing the posters. Not only does this create a learning experience for your helpers, but it also saves you time. Mount the posters around the room with masking tape. If tape would damage the walls, attach the signs to the chalkboard and to easels. If you use multiple posters, do not mount them in neat rows. Posters mounted at various angles and positions are more effective in getting learners' attention.
- Prepare other learning aids needed for the session. Obtain other materials you will need.
- Make any assignments well in advance. Be sure the person understands the assignment and knows where to find help in preparing it.
- Determine how members will make up missed sessions. Emphasize the importance of attending. But when absences occur, you will need to determine the best way for you and members to make up the sessions. Some possibilities include spending time yourself with the persons before the next session, having someone else accept this responsibility, or allowing their personal work to suffice. The third option is least acceptable.
- Commit your teaching plans to God and ask Him to lead during the session. Pray each day for each member of the group.

Tips on Leading and Facilitating

You will want to do everything possible to heighten the learning in each session. Here are some practical suggestions that will help you facilitate the study.

- Your job is not to teach the material to group members! The *Parent's Guide* is self-instructional, and you do not need to repeat everything the parent has already learned from working through the *Parent's Guide.* Your job as facilitator is to encourage and lead members in debriefing, sharing experiences, discussing problems and opportunities, and looking ahead to the next lesson. The learning that takes place during the group session builds on what parents have already learned from the *Parent's Guide* and what they have experienced in relating to their children.
- Arrange the meeting room properly before the session begins. The room arrangement should create an atmosphere conducive to learning. Seating should not physically exclude anyone.
- Arrive early to greet and talk with members as they arrive.
- Start and stop on time.
- Try to create a relaxed atmosphere that will help every member feel a sense of belonging. Use first names. Do not rush the activities.
- Encourage members to share their feelings, attitudes, insights, and experiences.
- Do not force the learning goals on members. Adapt and change them as necessary. Be sensitive to members' particular needs as you move through the study.
- Be alert to nonverbal signals. Be sensitive to the body language of the group. Who is withdrawn, bored, and so on?
- Be sure that you do not talk too much as facilitator. Do not be afraid of periods of silence.
- When you do talk, make what you say lively and interesting. Here are some helpful hints to keep in mind:

  —Use simple words.

  —Use the language of the learner.

  —Speak to the whole group.

  —Vary the voice pitch.

  —Emphasize the transition from one point to another.

  —Limit the number of points you wish to make.

  —Keep it short.

  —Use a bit of humor now and then.[1]
- Be flexible but do not allow the discussion to veer off on a tangent. Keep a focus on parenting by grace.
- Do not permit an overly talkative member to monopolize the discussion and sharing times. Consider these techniques: "Someone who has not already spoken, respond to the question." "Let's hear what someone else thinks about this." If necessary, go to the overly talkative person privately, thank him for his contributions, and then enlist his help in facilitating sharing by the entire group.
- Be an encourager. Show a caring, loving spirit.
- Be sensitive and alert to the need and opportunities to contact members between sessions. A telephone call or a note of affirmation could contribute significantly to a person's growth and learning.
- Be enthusiastic!

Planning the Introductory Session

The introductory session is crucial to the entire course. This session has four basic functions:

1. Introducing the course and its content
2. Building relationships among group members
3. Gathering information about group members that will help you plan the rest of the course
4. Establishing initial group expectations

Parents will decide during the introductory session whether to participate in the course. More persons may attend this introductory session than will make a commitment to take the course. This is as it should be. Not everyone will have the time or commitment to invest in the course.

During the introductory session be sensitive to the needs of group members. Take care not to make persons feel guilty if they decide not to enroll in the course. Assure them that the course will be offered again in the future.

Introducing the Course

Whether or not the following questions are asked at the introductory session, use them to prepare yourself to provide adequate information about the course.

- Will we be encouraged to develop as a group?
- Will the facilitator encourage confidentiality within the group and support for one another?
- How will we be grouped for the course?
- Will one group or several be offered?

- Where and when will my group meet?
- Who will be the facilitator of my group?
- Will my needs as a parent be met by attending the sessions?
- If I am a single parent, will my needs be addressed? If everyone else has a spouse, will I feel left out?
- What is parenting by grace?
- Is parenting by grace a realistic and positive approach to parenting?
- What topics will the course address?
- How long will the course last?
- Will it be a theory course, or will the facilitator encourage us to share our experiences?
- How does this course relate to other areas of the church's ministry?
- What will be required of me to become a member of this group? What commitments must I make?
- How long will the assignments take to complete?
- Can I leave now if I do not want to make a commitment?
- What is my first assignment?
- If I miss a session for a good reason, how do I make up the work?
- How much will this course cost?
- Does my spouse have to attend with me?
- How will my children benefit from the concepts taught in the course?

Other questions will likely emerge during the introductory session. These questions are more important to the parent than is the content of the introductory session. Be aware that while you are dealing with the content, you are also answering many of these questions.

Building Relationships and Gathering Information

Besides deciding whether they want to continue in the course, during this session parents will begin developing their way of relating to one another. Will we talk to one another or just ask questions of the group leader? To whom will I be able to feel close? You will need to learn as much as you can about members in this initial session. In particular, you need to know the following.

In what ways will parents' similarities and differences affect the way the group works together? Members need to trust and feel close to one another in order to risk talking about their concerns about their children and parenting. The group is more likely to be trusting if parents say to themselves, *Some of these people are like me.* Important characteristics include

- religious beliefs (a non-Christian parent may feel isolated and different among Christians);
- education and socioeconomic status (a parent who has less than a high-school education may feel uncomfortable in a group of professional parents with advanced degrees);
- stage of the family life cycle (one parent with an infant may feel out of place if the other parents all have teenagers);
- parenting role (a single Sunday School teacher who becomes involved because she wants to learn more about building self-esteem in her students will need considerable support if all of the other participants are parents).

Differences in one or a few of these characteristics may provide for creativity and variety of perspectives in the group. A young parent may appreciate and learn from the stories and experiences of parents of older children. Parents may appreciate and support concerned adults, such as Sunday School teachers, who want to be significant caregivers for children even though they may not be biological parents.

Two keys will help you turn differences to creative use in the group. First, help parents who are different from one another build bridges based on other characteristics. For example, parents of teenagers and preschoolers may be quite alike in their beliefs about providing children with role models that break through traditional gender roles, in their concern over the role of violence and competition in children's games, and in the difficulty they may have providing adequate child care and after-school supervision. You can build bridges by pointing out these similarities.

A second key to using differences creatively is simply labeling them as differences, from which parents may be able to learn something about themselves. The message that you should communicate is that being different is acceptable and that we do not intend to get everyone to agree or to be exactly alike. Each parent can learn from the others. With this message you are modeling the kind of acceptance of differences that nurtures healthy self-esteem.

Do any parents have significant problems with their children? Some parents may be attracted to *Parenting by Grace: Discipline and Spiritual Growth* because they desperately need help with their children. Parents need to understand that this course will not provide them with family counseling if that is what they need. This does not mean that parents having difficulties with their children cannot benefit from the course. In fact, they may find much helpful guidance in the course and in relationships with other parents. However, they will not find the intense attention to specific problems that counseling offers.

Troubled parents can create two problems in your parents' group. First, they may dominate the group as they try to use it to get help with their problems. You will want to communicate at the beginning of the group to all participants that the group is not designed to resolve specific problems (such as drug abuse, sexual acting out, tantrums), even though they may find the sessions to help with troubles they are experiencing.

Second, the rest of the group may be frightened by one parent's apparently serious problems with a child. They may not know how to respond to the pain of a parent whose child periodically runs away from home or has been hospitalized for emotional problems or may feel that their issues are insignificant by comparison. You can keep one parent's problems from threatening the group by

- giving positive definitions to what they are experiencing: "No matter how upset and worried you are, you still have a great deal of hope for your child, or you wouldn't be here";
- communicating to the group and the parent that you are not ignoring the seriousness of the issue: "This sounds like more than we can help you with here. Let's talk after the group session";
- taking responsibility for getting the group back on course, even if it means interrupting: "Let me interrupt you here, Jim. I really appreciate your sharing what you are struggling with. I know that we will all be in prayer for one another as we face the problems and decisions before us. Jim, let's talk more after tonight's meeting. I wonder what some of the rest of you are hoping to accomplish in this course."

Even if you are a professional family therapist, the role of the group leader does not include providing family counseling or therapy. If you are qualified, arrange for time to offer help to a family after the course is completed or even for one or two sessions during the course. Of course, you may also decide that you can be a more effective leader if you keep the roles of the group leader and therapist distinct, in which case referral to another family therapist is appropriate. If you are not a family professional, your church staff can help you find appropriate help for a parent who needs it.

How many parents will participate? The size of the group will make a significant difference in how you structure the group. The larger the group, the more formal your plans will need to be and the more central you will need to be as a leader. Small groups of from 9 to 12 persons tend to have greater participation by members and more potential for developing close ties among members.

A large group also offers some advantages. There is not as much pressure to participate; some parents may choose to prepare, come, observe, and talk very little, though they receive much from the course. For those who are uncomfortable talking in a group, a large group may be more comfortable because they can remain quiet more easily. Large groups can also tolerate differences more easily, since there is probably much more diversity in the group and ties do not become as close.

Small groups are almost essential, however, for building intimacy and lasting ties, for learning and practicing skills, and for learning that will result in life changes. If you are working with a large group but want the benefits of small groups, consider breaking the group into permanent small workgroups for all discussions and activities besides your presentations. Participants may learn little about other parents in a large group, but they will have opportunities to develop group intimacy and active participation in small groups. This may work particularly well if the small groups are organized by the ages of participants' children.

Do the parents know one another? A group of nodding acquaintances will have quite different dynamics than a group composed of persons related either closely or distantly by blood or marriage. During the introductory session you will help parents decide together whether what they say in the group should remain private, and it is helpful to know how important this issue may be. For example, if you have two adult sisters in the group, as well as two of their cousins, they need to wrestle with what it will mean to talk about their parenting—and the parenting they experienced—with the others present.

How mature is the group? This question refers to two aspects of the group as a whole:

- The variety of skills in the group. Is the group made up of persons who have the necessary skills to work well together? For example, are some in the group able to lead, encourage, and excite others about the purposes of the group? Are some caregivers who are sensitive to others' feelings and needs and can help them put those feelings and needs into words? The more skillful the group is as a whole, the less you will have to do to develop an intimate, self-sustaining group. The less skillful the group, the more central and active your role will be.

- The commitment of the group. How committed are the members to one another and to the concepts of parenting by grace? Can you turn your attention as a leader to the actual content of the course? Or do you first need to help members capture a vision of what they can learn from the course and how they can serve and be served by others in the group?

What are the special learning needs of this group? Every group is different. The parents in your group will be writing what they hope to learn in this course in preparation for this introductory session. Although you may not be able to address all of these concerns, you will probably find ways to deal with at least most of them and will find resources parents can use for the needs that will not be addressed in the group.

In addition to the special learning needs of these parents, they will also come to you from varying parenting contexts. You will want to know these contexts so that your leadership can be sensitive to the situations in which they will try to apply the concepts of the course. Some examples of parenting contexts include

- parents of an only child or of large families;
- single parents;
- parents in troubled or separated marriages;
- adults who are not biological parents but who feel called to minister in the lives of children;
- parents working inside and outside the home;
- adoptive parents;
- foster parents;
- parents of children with special needs (mental, physical, and emotional handicaps or chronic illness);
- parents who themselves have special needs (mental, physical, and emotional handicaps or chronic illness);
- parents of differing ethnic and cultural backgrounds;
- parents who began their families early (teenage parents) or late (first-time parents over age 35);
- parents of twins.

Establishing Expectations

Group members have certain expectations for one another and for the leader as they work together. The following are expectations you will want to discuss during the introductory session.

Privacy. Many groups find it helpful to state at the beginning that what they share with one another is to be respected as confidential and not to be told to others outside the parenting group.

Starting and ending times. When will the group begin and end? Will you wait for latecomers, or will you start promptly? Will you finish material even if you run over the stated ending time? Or will you stop no matter where you are when the ending time comes? Such issues may sound minor, but they can spare hurt feelings later when the group starts without a parent who is late or stops by interrupting a parent in the middle of an interesting discussion.

Attendance. Regular attendance is important not only for the individual parent's learning but also for parents in the group who depend on other members for support, encouragement, and good ideas.

Homework. The sessions will be planned on the assumption that parents have read the *Parent's Guide* and have completed the exercises and activities in it.

Structure. How do we want the group structured? Do we want to be formal, with the leader as the hub of discussion, recognizing members and answering questions? Or do we want to be less formal, talking with one another and participating when we can?

Voluntary participation. How do we want to encourage members to share? Do we want to ask one another questions and expect everyone to have something to say? Do we want to push one another gently to participate, or does it strictly depend on each parent?

Some parents, after the introductory session, may decide that other demands in their personal, family, or professional lives would keep them from making the serious commitment of time and energy that participation in *Parenting by Grace: Discipline and Spiritual Growth* demands. Encourage them to use their best judgment in deciding whether to participate in the group at this time or prayerfully to reconsider participating in the course on another occasion.

—

[1]LeRoy Ford, *Using the Lecture in Teaching and Training* (Nashville: Broadman Press, 1968), 120-21.

Introductory Session

Session Goals

After completing this session, members should have a better understanding of parenting by grace as a concept and as the subject of this course. Members will be able to

- describe the purpose of *Parenting by Grace: Discipline and Spiritual Growth;*
- state two reasons why parenting is significant;
- list at least three trends in parenting;
- identify two needs they have as parents;
- define *grace;*
- explain the role of grace in parenting;
- make a commitment to complete this course.

Before the Session

1. Carefully study the introduction in the *Parent's Guide* and complete all of the personal learning activities.
2. Duplicate worksheets 1, 2, and 3.
3. Write the following statements on large sheets of newsprint with felt-tip markers. Mount the sheets in random order on the walls.
   - Parenting by grace is as timeless as God's plan for humankind.
   - Parents have the first opportunity to influence their children.
   - Parents' influence on children is immeasurable.
   - Parenting is an awesome responsibility.
   - Our Heavenly Father parents us by grace.
   - Sharing and caring are risky.
   - Grace is the free, unconditional gift of love and mercy from God.
   - God gives His love and mercy to Christians with no strings attached.
   - The clearest example of God's grace is seen in the coming of Jesus Christ.
   - "Jesus kept increasing in wisdom and stature, and in favor with God and men" (Luke 2:52, NASB).
   - Mary and Joseph provided the earthly parenting for God's only Son.
   - Children are gifts from God.
4. Have copies of the *Parent's Guide* available for participants.
5. Have blank name tags (if needed), markers, and registration materials available. Also get a *Parenting by Grace: Discipline and Spiritual Growth* Church Study Course Diploma to show.
6. Make a poster that lists all of the unit and session titles. Make this poster as large as possible. You will display it in every session. Prepare a one-by-four-inch poster-board arrow. Color it and glue a wooden clothespin to the back of it. Clip this to the outline poster to point to the appropriate lesson.
7. Obtain an ample supply of newspapers (various issues).
8. Pray for those who will attend the session as well as for yourself as leader.

During the Session

1. Arrive early. Greet members as they arrive, asking them to make name tags if they do not know one another. Distribute copies of worksheet 1 and ask members to begin work on it.
2. After most members have finished the group work described on worksheet 1, greet members and welcome them to the session. Explain that this session will introduce the course and will provide an opportunity later for members to make commitments to complete the course.
3. Lead in prayer.

PRESENTATION

4. Explain that *Parenting by Grace: Discipline and Spiritual Growth* is a part of the LIFE (Lay Institute for Equipping) learning system. Tell members that the course has three distinctive features: (1) individual study and completion of the *Parent's Guide* at home, (2) on-the-job experience implementing the guidelines and principles of parenting by grace with their children, and (3) group sessions to discuss and reflect on their learning.
5. Explain that Church Study Course credit will be given for the course. Show the *Parenting by Grace: Discipline and Spiritual Growth* Diploma and encourage members to earn it by completing the course.
6. Share the general learning goal for the course: The purpose of *Parenting by Grace: Discipline and Spiritual Growth* is to help you become a better parent. Use the information in "The Purpose of Parenting by Grace" on page 13 in the *Parent's Guide* to share ways the course will help members.
7. Use the outline poster to overview the entire course. Emphasize the importance of members' completing the lessons before the group sessions. Also empha-

size the importance of putting into practice what is learned.

8. Give each member a copy of the *Parent's Guide.* Ask members to turn to the topic "Significance of Parenting" on page 13. Use this material as an example of the interactive nature of the study material. Ask members to read the topic and to do the underlining and writing requested. Allow three minutes for this activity. Then ask members to turn through the *Parent's Guide* and to note the many activities that call for involvement. Emphasize again the importance of being actively involved with the study material.
9. Call attention to "Trends in Parenting" on page 14 in the *Parent's Guide.* Divide members into small groups of three or four persons each. Distribute newspapers and ask each small group to search for trends in parenting. Allow a few minutes for small-group work and call for reports.
10. Ask members to complete the evaluation of family needs on page 15 in the *Parent's Guide.* Allow a few minutes for individual work and then lead members to name their greatest family needs. Be sensitive, remembering that because this is a new group, members may not be ready to open up and share at an intimate interpersonal level.
11. Write the word *grace* on the chalkboard. Ask members to call out their definitions of the term. Briefly summarize the biblical concept of grace and the example of Mary and Joseph in parenting (p. 16 in the *Parent's Guide*).
12. Point out "Parenting by Grace Presuppositions" on page 16 in the *Parent's Guide.*
13. Distribute copies of worksheet 2 and ask each member to share responses with a partner.
14. Calling attention to the commitment activity on page 17 in the *Parent's Guide,* ask members to make the commitment. Again, recognize that everyone may not be ready to invest the amount of time and work required for the course. Lead in a prayer of commitment.
15. Refer to the teaching posters on the walls. Ask volunteers to read and comment on the meanings of the signs. These signs review and summarize the lesson.

PREVIEW AND ASSIGNMENT

16. Briefly preview lesson 1.
17. Ask members to complete at home the activities in "Looking Ahead" on page 18 in the *Parent's Guide.*
18. Ask members to read lesson 1 and to complete all of the learning activities.
19. Distribute copies of worksheet 3 and ask members to complete the pretest at home.
20. Close with another prayer, asking God to guide the study.

After the Session

1. Carefully evaluate the effectiveness of the session by answering the following questions.
   - Do you believe that members achieved the learning goals?
   - Did you lead the session in an orderly manner?
   - Did you have a dominant role as a lecturer during the session, or did you serve as a facilitator to involve members in discussion?
   - Were all members involved in the learning activities?
   - Did you show a genuine interest in each member of the group? What could have been done to create more interest and participation?
   - Did the logistics move smoothly (handing out worksheets, moving into and out of groups, and so on)?
   - What could have been done to improve the session?
2. What did you learn from the session that you should remember and use as you plan for the next session?
3. Do you need to make any personal contacts or follow up with any member of the group?
4. Save the outline poster for use in the remaining sessions.
5. Pray for members between sessions.

WORKSHEET 1

Begin work as soon as you receive this worksheet.

1. Just for fun, complete the following sentence: Sometimes being a parent is like

____

2. Write words describing your child that begin with the following letters.

C ____

H ____

I ____

L ____

D ____

Find someone other than your spouse and compare the ways you described your children.

3. You and your partner find another set of partners and form a small group of four. Spend a few moments getting acquainted. Talk about your families, providing such information as:
   - How many were in your family when you were a child?

   ____

   - What are the names and ages of your children?

   ____

   ____

   - In what ways was your childhood different from that of your children?

   ____

   ____

4. Spend a few moments of quiet reflection before answering the following questions. After about two minutes each person in the group should share his answers with the others. Begin with the parent with the oldest child and continue to the left.
   - What one word would you use to describe your childhood? ____________________
   - More than anything, what would you like to gain from this parent-enrichment course?

   ____

   ____

WORKSHEET 2

Work with a partner to respond to these questions.

1. What are some modern-day pressures on your family?

____

2. What one thing causes the most pressure on your family?

____

3. Why do you think it is so difficult to raise children in today's culture and society?

____

4. Do your children know that your love for them is unconditional?

____

5. How has being a parent helped you grow?

____

6. What is your definition of *grace?*

____

7. What are some ways you experience God's grace in your life?

____

8. What are some ways your children have seen God's grace at work in your life?

____

9. What is one significant difference between the family makeup of Mary and Joseph's home and that of our homes today?

____

10. What are your feelings about this course at this time?

____

WORKSHEET 3

Test your knowledge of parenting by grace by completing the pretest. Mark each statement *T* (true) or *F* (false). At the end of the course you will be asked to take this test again to see what you have learned.

Pretest	Posttest	
______	______	1. Unconditional love is essential in parenting by grace.
______	______	2. Affirmation does not work with preschoolers.
______	______	3. Discipline and punishment are synonymous.
______	______	4. Discipline focuses on past misbehavior.
______	______	5. The rate of development varies little from one child to another.
______	______	6. The development of children proceeds in stages.
______	______	7. The development of children builds on the previous stages of development.
______	______	8. Young children do not think in abstract terms.
______	______	9. The process of maturity is less influenced by the environment than is learning.
______	______	10. *Learning* can be defined as a change in behavior or attitude.
______	______	11. Discipline is harmful to a child's development.
______	______	12. Parenting by grace is a set of parenting methods to be used with a child.
______	______	13. The goal of discipline in parenting is to help the child develop self-discipline.
______	______	14. Appropriate behavior for children is a matter of moral absolutes and does not depend on parental expectations.
______	______	15. Children who receive affirmation as the main kind of discipline do not resist temptation as effectively as children who are punished for misbehavior.
______	______	16. Praise from others could cause a child to be more vulnerable to inappropriate suggestions from others.
______	______	17. Reinforcement should match a child's age.
______	______	18. A child's expression of feelings should not be reinforced.
______	______	19. Specific praise is less effective than general praise.
______	______	20. A teachable moment is an opportunity the parent has to discipline the child.
______	______	21. Discussion is better than lecturing to children.
______	______	22. The church has the primary responsibility to teach spiritual and moral values to children.
______	______	23. Teachable moments cannot be created.
______	______	24. Modeling as a parenting technique means that the parent is an example the child strives to imitate.
______	______	25. The three primary models in children's lives are parents, peers, and teachers.

UNIT 1

Grace: God's Gift to Parents and Children

Session 1

Love and Affirmation

Session Goals

After completing this session, members should better understand the importance and use of love and affirmation in the parenting process. Members will be able to

- define *love* and *affirmation* as related to parenting;
- summarize in their own words what the Bible teaches about love and affirmation as expressed in parenting;
- state three ways they can show love and affirmation for their children;
- state at least four principles of love and affirmation that apply to parenting;
- affirm their children on a regular basis.

Before the Session

1. Carefully study lesson 1 and complete all of the personal learning activities.
2. Duplicate worksheets 4, 5, 6, 7, 8, and 9.
3. Write the following statements on large sheets of newsprint with felt-tip markers. Mount them in random order on the walls around the room.
    - "God is love" (1 John 4:8).
    - Children need parents to validate their worth.
    - God expects parents to express love and compassion toward their children.
    - Only those who know God's love through Christ have a foundation for parenting by grace.
    - "Let the children come to me"—a beautiful expression of love and affirmation!
    - Open arms, open hearts, and open ears say, "I love you" to children with signals loud and clear.
    - God loves us; therefore, we are of great value and infinite worth.
    - Children's needs are best met by parents whose needs are met.
    - God has chosen to give His love and mercy to us with no strings attached.
    - Unconditional love does not mean your child is free to do anything.
    - No family's life together is smooth sailing all the time.
    - Actions speak louder than words.
4. Prepare three word strips on the ways to show love and affirmation: (1) being accessible, (2) being willing to learn from children, (3) following the biblical example of blessing.

During the Session

1. Greet members as they arrive. Begin with prayer.

DEBRIEFING

2. Briefly review the introductory session, referring to "Summary" on pages 17–18 in the *Parent's Guide.* Emphasize grace as the foundation of parenting and the parenting-by-grace presuppositions.
3. Ask if members had difficulty completing worksheet 3 but do not discuss the answers. Instruct members to keep the pretest until the end of the course, explaining that they will take the test again to determine what they have learned.
4. Involve members in a discussion of the activities they completed in "Looking Ahead" in the introductory session (p. 18 in the *Parent's Guide*). Consider these questions:
    - Is *love* the one word that best describes your childhood? What other words come to mind in

describing your childhood?

- How was your childhood similar to or different from your children's childhood?
- Which age-group activity did you complete? How was the activity received by your child?

5. Give members an opportunity to share any experiences they had between sessions applying what they learned.

PRESENTATION

6. Use "Overview" on page 20 in the *Parent's Guide* to introduce this session on love and affirmation. Review the learning goals for the session.
7. Distribute copies of worksheet 4 and allow time for completion. Allow time for discussion as answers are shared. These statements summarize the entire session and allow the content to be presented in an interesting format. Be sure to bring out any points and background material not covered in the discussion. Suggested responses based on the material: 1. D, 2. D, 3. A, 4. A, 5. A, 6. D, 7. D, 8. A, 9. D, 10. A.

SKILL DEVELOPMENT

8. Mount the three word strips on the wall or chalkboard. Involve members in discussing practical ways to implement these guidelines or ways to show love and affirmation. Encourage parents to share from their personal experiences.
9. Distribute copies of worksheet 5. Ask a volunteer to read Galatians 5:22-26. Relate this passage to the first principle of love and affirmation. Allow time for members to complete the worksheet. Then give an opportunity for sharing and discussion.
10. Distribute copies of worksheet 6. Relate it to the principle of loving self and having a healthy self-concept. Allow time for sharing, based on the five questions.
11. Distribute copies of worksheet 7. Relate it to the principle of unconditionally loving your children. Lead members in discussing the statements. Ask members to share examples of having followed or violated this principle. Answers: 1. C, 2. C, 3. U, 4. U, 5. U, 6. C, 7. C, 8. U, 9. C, 10. U.
12. Distribute copies of worksheet 8. Relate it to the unique personality and developmental characteristics of children. Do not take time to complete it during the session but ask members to complete it at home. Ask, What are some practical actions we can take to show more respect for the actions of our children? List actions on the chalkboard as members respond. Ask members to keep worksheet 8 for use again in session 5.
13. Distribute copies of worksheet 9. Ask each member to keep a record this week of the amount of time he or she spends with each child each day.
14. Spend a few minutes discussing the chart of "I" messages and "you" messages on page 25 in the *Parent's Guide.* Ask members to share what they learned from using the chart.
15. If time permits, involve members in discussing the first four questions and statements under "Reflection and Application" on page 25 in the *Parent's Guide.*
16. Summarize by calling attention to the teaching poster "God expects parents to express love and compassion toward their children."

PREVIEW AND ASSIGNMENT

17. Briefly preview lesson 2. Use the outline poster prepared before the introductory session to show how the lessons relate to and build on one another.
18. Ask members to complete at home the activities in "Looking Ahead" on page 26 in the *Parent's Guide.*
19. Close with prayer.

After the Session

Refer to "After the Session" on page 26 in this guide.

WORKSHEET 4

Mark each statement *A* (agree) or *D* (disagree).

____ 1. God should be referred to as Father with children who have poor relationships with their parents.

____ 2. God's purposes are determined by the attitude and actions of people.

____ 3. Love and affirmation are communicated to children by the accessibility of their parents.

____ 4. Parents should give their children gifts that have personal or family meaning behind them.

____ 5. A right relationship with God is essential for effective parenting.

____ 6. Self-love works against effective parenting.

____ 7. Unconditional love tends to spoil a child.

____ 8. The older the child, the more appropriate verbal guidance becomes.

____ 9. Comparing a child's accomplishments with those of other children is an effective way of motivating the child to greater achievement.

____ 10. "I" messages are less threatening than "you" messages.

WORKSHEET 5

Read Galatians 5:22-26. Spend a few minutes reflecting on evidences of the fruit of the Spirit in your life as you relate to your children. Evaluate how you feel about your life in relationship to the gift. Circle a number for each.

	Poor				Excellent
Love	1	2	3	4	5
Joy	1	2	3	4	5
Peace	1	2	3	4	5
Patience	1	2	3	4	5
Kindness	1	2	3	4	5
Goodness	1	2	3	4	5
Faithfulness	1	2	3	4	5
Gentleness	1	2	3	4	5
Self-control	1	2	3	4	5

Now evaluate yourself in terms of how you think your children would rate you in relation to each. If you have more than one child, put each child's initial over the number he or she would give you for each.

Which areas of your life need special attention?

____

____

____

____

What specific actions can you take to strengthen those areas?

____

____

____

____

WORKSHEET 6

Children's needs are best met by parents whose needs are met. Evaluate your life in each of the four areas shown on the following grid. Number 1 is weak, and 7 is healthy and strong. Place *X* on each line according to your evaluation. Then connect the four *X*s with lines.

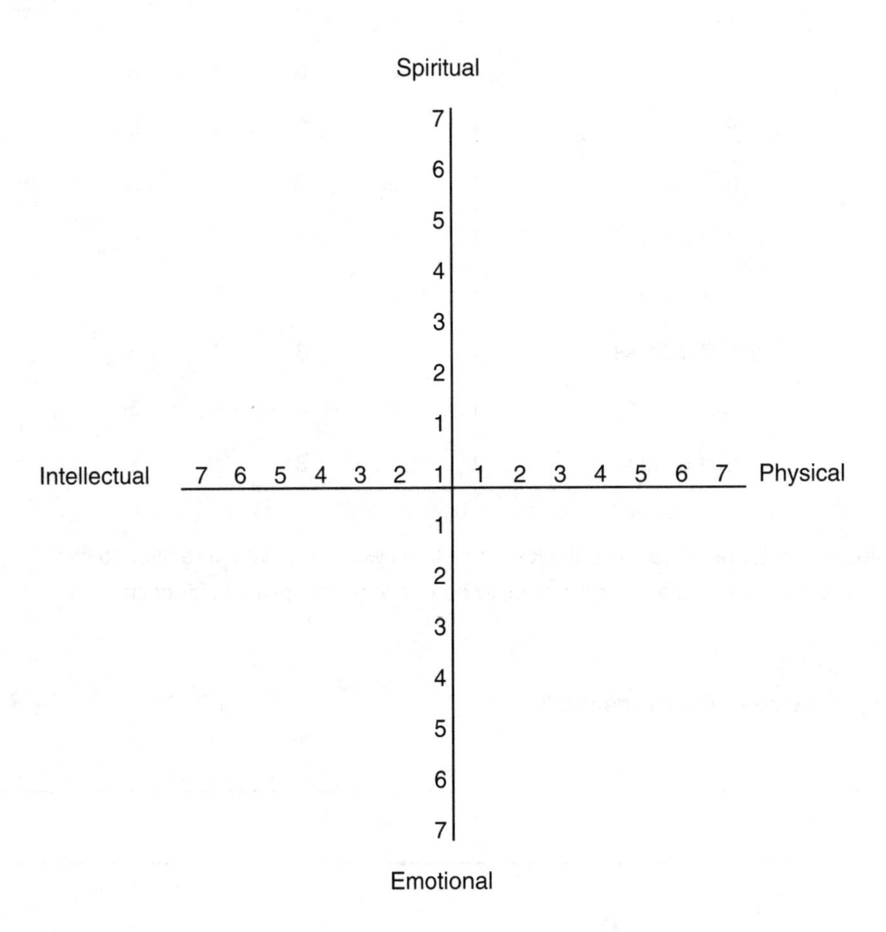

1. Are your lines balanced or lopsided? ______________________________

2. Are your lines small or large? ______________________________

3. Which of the four areas is strongest? ______________________________

4. Which of the four areas is weakest? ______________________________

5. What is one action you can take to improve in your weakest area? ______________________________

WORKSHEET 7

As you read each statement, decide whether it is characteristic of conditional or unconditional love. Place *C* in the blank beside each statement describing conditional love and *U* beside each statement describing unconditional love.

___ 1. "You're such a good girl; Mommy loves you when you are good!"

___ 2. "We're so proud to be your parents when you play football as you did tonight!"

___ 3. "It doesn't matter if you made cheerleader or not, Sweetheart."

___ 4. "I know you didn't mean to break my necklace. Come here and let me hug you."

___ 5. "You shouldn't have stayed out past curfew, son. You're grounded for a week. But you know we're doing this only because we care about you."

___ 6. "If you want me to be good to you, you'd better behave!"

___ 7. "I love you so much when you sit quietly in church."

___ 8. "We think you're making a mistake to quit school and move into your own apartment; but remember, you'll always have a home with us."

___ 9. "I'm glad to tell people you're mine because you're so smart and pretty."

___ 10. "I love you just because you're you!"

Write a brief explanation of the difference between conditional and unconditional love.

___

___

___

___

___

___

___

___

WORKSHEET 8

Complete the following personality profile for your children. Write the name of each child in the columns across the top. Place a check mark beside each adjective that describes the child.

Names						
Calm						
Carefree						
Cautious						
Compliant						
Dependent						
Dominant						
Expressive						
Flexible						
Independent						
Intense						
Loud						
Loving						
Neat						
Nervous						
Outgoing						
Passive						
Quiet						
Relaxed						
Reserved						
Rigid						
Self-reliant						
Shy						
Sloppy						
Sociable						
Solitary						
Strong-willed						

How can you show more respect for the uniqueness of your children?

____

____

WORKSHEET 9

Keep a record this week of the amount of time you spend with each of your children each day. On the chart below write the name of each child in the columns across the top. Write the amount of time in the appropriate box for each day.

Names					
Sunday					
Monday					
Tuesday					
Wednesday					
Thursday					
Friday					
Saturday					

Session 2

Discipline and Guidance

Session Goals

After completing this session, members should better understand the nature and use of discipline and guidance in the parenting process. Members will be able to

- define *discipline* as related to parenting;
- summarize in their own words what the Bible teaches about discipline and guidance as expressed in parenting;
- state at least four principles of discipline and guidance that apply to parenting;
- explain the difference between discipline and punishment;
- identify one behavioral problem or pattern with their children that requires discipline;
- outline plans for disciplining their children in response to the behavioral problem identified.

Before the Session

1. Carefully study lesson 2 and complete all of the learning activities.
2. Duplicate worksheets 10 and 11 and case studies 1 and 2.
3. Write the following statements on large sheets of newsprint. Mount them in random order on the walls around the room.
   - The goal of discipline is to guide our children to become self-controlled.
   - Parental love needs to include discipline.
   - Love and discipline are closely related.
   - To fail to discipline proves a lack of parental love.
   - "Train up a child in the way he should go" (Prov. 22:6).
   - Sensitive listening is the starting point for meeting needs.
   - We need to relearn the value of a kind, considerate approach.
   - "A soft answer turneth away wrath" (Prov. 15:1).
   - Does your home have that lived-in look?
   - We should care enough to set appropriate limits.
   - Consistency is a key to discipline.
   - Limits provide reassurance for children.

During the Session

1. Welcome members. Ask someone to lead in prayer.

DEBRIEFING

2. Briefly review lesson 1, referring to "Summary" on page 26 in the *Parent's Guide.*
3. Involve members in a discussion of the activities they completed in "Looking Ahead" in lesson 1 (p. 26 in the *Parent's Guide*). Ask these questions:
   - How were you challenged to show God's characteristics in your relationships with your children?
   - How can you begin to respond to the most difficult problem you face in disciplining your children?
   - How have your childhood experiences with punishment influenced your role as a parent?
   - What were the results of trying methods of discipline and guidance, other than punishment, with your children this week?
4. Ask members to share their time logs (worksheet 9) with partners, indicating the amount of time they spent each day with each child. Ask members to identify strengths, weaknesses, and discernible patterns in the time records.

PRESENTATION

5. Call attention to the learning goals for the session.
6. Write the word *discipline* on the chalkboard. Ask members to call out all of the synonyms they can think of as you list them on the chalkboard. Briefly summarize what the Bible teaches about discipline and guidance. Ask for responses to the four agree/disagree statements on page 28 in the *Parent's Guide.* Ask members to share the symbols they drew for discipline in "The Bible Speaks to Discipline and Guidance" (p. 29 in the *Parent's Guide*).
7. Distribute copies of worksheet 10 and allow time for completion. Allow time for discussion as answers are shared. Suggested responses: 1. D, 2. D, 3. A, 4. D, 5. D, 6. A, 7. A, 8. D, 9. D, 10. A.
8. Lead a brief discussion of the contrast between punishment and discipline. Refer to the chart on page 32 in the *Parent's Guide.*
9. Call attention to the nine principles of discipline and guidance. Refer to the list of principles in "Summary" on page 33 in the *Parent's Guide.* Ask members to circle a key word in each principle. Then ask one person to call out a key word and someone else to identify the principle involved.

SKILL DEVELOPMENT

10. Distribute copies of worksheet 11 and allow time for completion. Ask members to share in pairs their areas of strength and weakness. Then involve the entire group in a discussion of specific actions they can take to improve in using the principles.
11. Divide members into groups of three and give each group one of the two case studies. Allow time for group work and call for reports.
12. Refer to the chart in activity 6 of "Reflection and Application" (p. 33 in the *Parent's Guide*). Discuss the methods of discipline and results; then ask members to share their experiences with the various methods.
13. Ask members to share their responses to activities 4 and 5 in "Reflection and Application" on page 33 in the *Parent's Guide.*
14. Summarize the session by asking members to read aloud the teaching posters and to comment on their meanings.

PREVIEW AND ASSIGNMENT

15. Preview lesson 3 by using the outline poster.
16. Ask members to complete at home the activities in "Looking Ahead" on page 33 in the *Parent's Guide.*
17. Close with prayer.

After the Session

Refer to "After the Session" on page 26 in this guide.

WORKSHEET 10

Mark each statement *A* (agree) or *D* (disagree).

D 1. Physical punishment should never be used with children.

D 2. Parental permissiveness communicates love and concern to a child.

A 3. Limits are reassuring to children.

D 4. Limits are not necessary with older teens.

D 5. Discipline and punishment are synonymous.

A 6. Punishment tends to lead children to remain dependent on others to direct their lives.

A 7. Children eventually tend to believe caustic, harsh words directed toward them.

D 8. Preschoolers are too young to make choices.

D 9. Punishment focuses on self-discipline.

A 10. A parent should not discipline a child when the parent is angry.

WORKSHEET 11

Evaluate yourself on the following principles of discipline and guidance.

	Weak				Strong
1. I try to understand the development of my child.	1	2	3	4	5
2. I listen to my child.	1	2	3	4	5
3. I am a good observer of my child's behavior.	1	2	3	4	5
4. I speak to my child kindly and quietly, yet firmly.	1	2	3	4	5
5. I speak on my child's level.	1	2	3	4	5
6. My home is childproof.	1	2	3	4	5
7. I identify appropriate limits for my child.	1	2	3	4	5
8. I consistently maintain necessary limits.	1	2	3	4	5
9. I encourage my child's development of freedom within limits.	1	2	3	4	5

Two areas in which I am very strong are:

____

____

Two areas in which I need to improve are:

____

____

One specific action I can take to improve in my weak areas is:

____

____

____

____

Case Study 1

Analyze the following case study.

Your seven-year-old daughter has terrible table manners every time guests come for dinner. She interrupts while others are talking, she eats with her fingers, and she gulps down her food.

1. Which principles of discipline and guidance apply most directly to this situation? How would you use these principles to deal with the problem?

   Principles that apply to this situation:

   How I would use the principles:

2. Outline how you would approach and deal with this situation.

Case Study 2

Analyze the following case study.

Your 14-year-old son has poor study habits. He rarely brings any books home. His teacher has sent you a note saying that your son has not been turning in his assigned homework. When you confront your son with the problem, he says: "School is boring. I don't like it."

1. Which principles of discipline and guidance apply most directly to this situation? How would you use these principles to deal with the problem?

   Principles that apply to this situation:

   How I would use the principles:

2. Outline how you would approach and deal with this situation.

UNIT 2

Helping Children Grow According to God's Plan

Session 3

Physical, Moral, and Spiritual Development

Session Goals

After completing this session, members should have a better understanding of the physical, moral, and spiritual development of their children. They will be able to

- select from a given list of definitions the correct ones for *growth, maturation,* and *learning;*
- describe briefly the typical characteristics of the developmental stages of their children;
- name three persons a parent must know in order to parent by grace;
- identify from a list of developmental needs the ones to which they need to give special attention in order to help their children develop;
- take two specific actions to help their children more effectively in their development.

Before the Session

1. Carefully study lesson 3 and complete all of the learning activities.
2. Duplicate worksheets 12, 13, and 14.
3. Write the following statements on large sheets of newsprint. Mount them in random order on the walls around the room.
   - Development is the result of the interaction of growth, maturation, and learning.
   - Growth is quantitative change.
   - Maturation is qualitative change.
   - The order of development varies little.
   - The rate of development varies greatly.
   - Development proceeds in stages.
   - Development is cumulative.
   - Learning to trust parents is basic for all relationships.
   - The foundation for a child's life is laid in the first three years.
   - Children learn not by what we say but by what we do.
   - Parents need to parent their children as gifts from God.

During the Session

1. Distribute copies of worksheet 12 to members as they arrive and ask them to complete it before the session begins.
2. Give an opportunity for members to share prayer requests. Ask someone to lead in prayer.

DEBRIEFING

3. Briefly review lesson 2, using "Summary" on page 33 in the *Parent's Guide.*
4. Lead members in a discussion of the activities they completed in "Looking Ahead" in lesson 2 (p. 33 in the *Parent's Guide*). Ask these questions:
   - What are some specific examples of lessons your child is learning about God from his relationship with you?
   - What attitudes and behaviors do you need to change to correct unwanted perceptions your child is gaining?
   - How can you begin to make those changes?
   - What did you discover about your child as you wrote a description of his or her level of development at this time?
   - Do you have reasonable expectations for your child's behavior at this time?

- How effectively are you communicating these "just right" expectations to your child?

PRESENTATION

5. State the learning goals for this session.
6. Distribute copies of worksheet 13 and allow three minutes for members to complete it. Ask volunteers to read the statements aloud. As each statement is read, ask members who agree with the statement to raise their hands. Then determine those who disagree and those who are undecided. If the group is divided in opinion, allow some time for discussion of the statement. Do this by allowing a representative of the "agree" group to speak for 20 seconds, explaining his or her position. Then allow someone from the "disagree" group equal time to speak on his or her position. This process can create a great deal of interest and discussion as you move into a study of lesson 3. Here are our responses to the statements: 1. D, 2. A, 3. D, 4. A, 5. A, 6. D, 7. A, 8. D, 9. D, 10. A, 11. D, 12. A, 13. A.
7. Refer to worksheet 12, completed as a presession activity. Lead in a discussion as the answers are shared (1. order, 2. maturation, 3. learning, 4. cumulative, 5. development, 6. preschool, 7. adolescence, 8. rate, 9. special, 10. rules, 11. growth, 12. God, 13. example, 14. infancy).
8. Distribute copies of worksheet 14 and allow time for completion. Lead in a discussion as answers are shared (1. d, 2. c, 3. b, 4. e, 5. c, 6. a, 7. e, 8. d, 9. a, 10. e).

SKILL DEVELOPMENT

9. Refer to the four teaching posters that state the four principles of child development. (The order of development varies little. The rate of development varies greatly. Development proceeds in stages. Development is cumulative.) Ask members to share evidences or illustrations of these principles from the lives of their children.
10. Refer to the five stages of child development (infancy, preschool, early childhood, late childhood, and adolescence). Discuss them briefly, using these questions:
    - Do these stages of child development help you understand your child? If so, in what ways?
    - What are some ways your child differs from the typical characteristics of the stages?
11. Emphasize the importance of having a living relationship with God in order to be an effective parent. Refer to the self-evaluation on page 38 in the *Parent's Guide.* Ask members to share in pairs one strong area and one weak area in their lives from the evaluation. Close this activity by asking members to pray sentence prayers.
12. Form three small groups according to age groups of members' children (preschoolers, elementary age, adolescents). Ask members to use the charts in "Needs of Children," beginning on page 38 in the *Parent's Guide,* as the basis of their sharing. Write these points on the chalkboard to help guide the small-group sharing:
    - The extent to which my child's needs are being met
    - Special needs my child has that are not listed on the chart
    - Unique needs of my child because of his being a special child, my being a single parent, or our being a blended family
    - Needs I should give special attention in order to help my child develop
13. Refer to the two charts on affirmation and celebration and on discipline and guidance, pages 41–42 in the *Parent's Guide.* Allow a few minutes for members to share their experiences in these two areas during the past week.
14. Summarize the session by asking members to read aloud the teaching posters and to comment on their meanings.

PREVIEW AND ASSIGNMENT

15. Preview lesson 4 by using the outline poster.
16. Ask members to complete at home the activity in "Looking Ahead" on page 42 in the *Parent's Guide.*
17. Close with prayer.

After the Session

Refer to "After the Session" on page 26 in this guide.

WORKSHEET 12

Refer to lesson 3 as needed to complete this crossword puzzle.

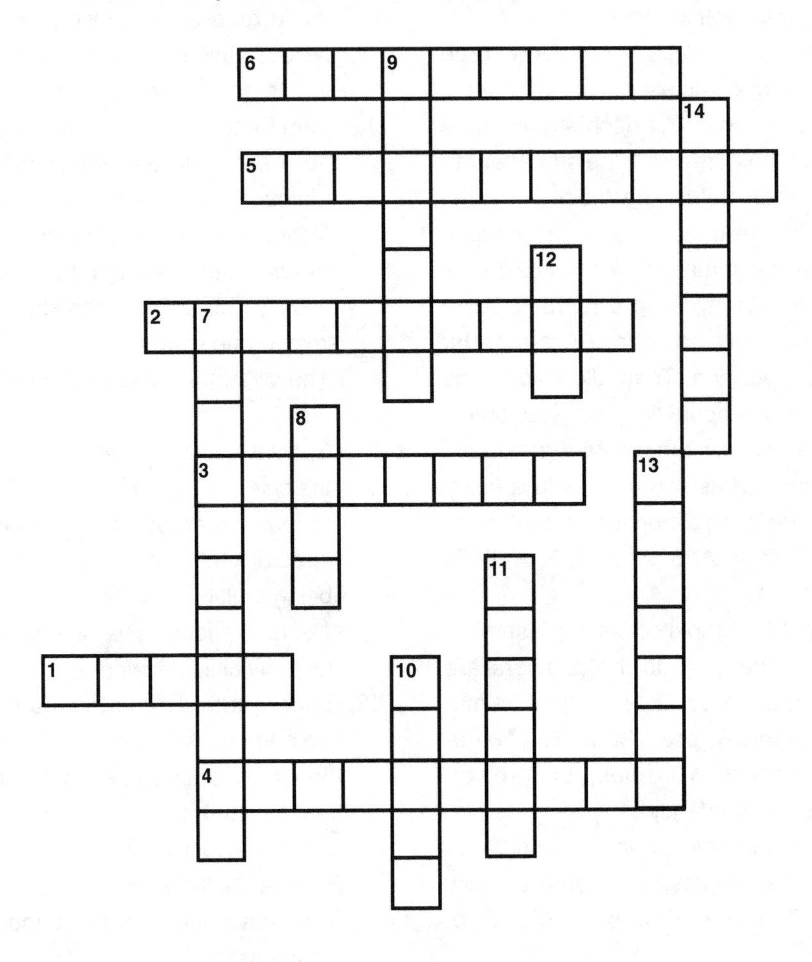

Across

1. This aspect of development varies little from one child to another.
2. A term used to refer to qualitative changes in a person.
3. A term used to describe a change in behavior or attitude.
4. A word used to show that one stage of development builds on the previous stages.
5. Occurs as the result of the interaction of growth, maturation, and learning.
6. The developmental stage in which the child is extremely self-centered.

Down

7. Radical changes take place in cognitive or thinking abilities during this developmental stage.
8. This aspect of development varies greatly from one child to another.
9. A word used to describe children with handicaps or gifts.
10. These are very important to children in early childhood.
11. A term generally used to describe the more obvious, tangible, concrete changes in children's lives.
12. Whom parents must know in order to parent effectively.
13. A primary way by which children learn.
14. The developmental stage from birth to two.

WORKSHEET 13

Read each statement. If you agree with the statement, write *A* in the blank. If you disagree with the statement, write *D.* If you are undecided, write *U.*

__ 1. Learning is influenced less by the environment than by maturation.

__ 2. Almost all children sit before they stand.

__ 3. The rate of development varies little with special children.

__ 4. Babies learn primarily through sensory experiences.

__ 5. Security helps a child develop independence.

__ 6. Older children are more dependent than younger children on rewards and punishment to shape their behavior.

__ 7. Young children do not think in abstract terms.

__ 8. Preschoolers are too young to learn how to relate to others.

__ 9. Elementary-age children are too young to have personal relationships with Christ.

__ 10. Teens need guidance in career decisions.

__ 11. Self-esteem is a low-priority need of special children.

__ 12. Children of blended families often have problems in the areas of relationships and communication.

__ 13. Many children have unique needs that cross age- and stage-development categories.

WORKSHEET 14

Match each characteristic with its correct developmental stage.

__ 1. Depend less on rewards and punishment to shape their behavior.

__ 2. Obey rules to avoid parent and teacher disapproval and to gain acceptance.

__ 3. Take first steps from self-centeredness to God-centeredness.

__ 4. Radical physical changes take place.

__ 5. Move beyond themselves to the world and try to understand it.

__ 6. Learn first lessons about the nature of God through experiences with those who care (or do not care) for them.

__ 7. Think in abstract terms.

__ 8. Their faith is becoming their own rather than something mediated through parents.

__ 9. Learn primarily through sensory experiences of taste, touch, sound, sight, and smell.

__ 10. Periods of turbulence and upheaval alternate with confidence and sunshine.

a. Infancy (birth–2 years)

b. Preschool (ages 2–5)

c. Early childhood (ages 6–9)

d. Late childhood (ages 10–11)

e. Adolescence (ages 12–17)

Session 4

Discipline Grows Children in the Way They Should Go

Session Goals

After completing this session, members should better understand the use of discipline in the parenting process. They will be able to

- summarize in their own words the value of discipline in parenting;
- state five additional basic principles not discussed in lesson 2;
- summarize briefly in their own words what the Bible teaches about parental responsibility for discipline;
- identify the cause of one behavioral problem or pattern in their children previously identified in lesson 2;
- implement at least two basic principles of discipline with their children.

Before the Session

1. Carefully study lesson 4 and complete all of the learning activities.
2. Duplicate worksheets 15 and 16 and case studies 3, 4, 5, and 6.
3. Write the following statements on large sheets of newsprint. Mount them in random order on the walls around the room.
   - Discipline grows children in the way they should go.
   - Good discipline encourages each person to find himself in God.
   - Discipline helps children learn self-discipline.
   - No easy answers or definite rules exist to make us loving, merciful parents.
   - Parenting by grace is an attitude.
   - All of life influences the spiritual and moral development of a child.
   - The goal of Christian parenting is to bring children to mature, responsible Christian living.
   - We are not in the parenting task alone.
   - Parents have the joy of participating in their child's life.
   - The principles found in the Bible are ageless.
   - God's grace accepts us no matter what we do.
   - God gave us the perfect example of unconditional love in Jesus Christ.
   - Punishment comes from anger; discipline comes from love.
   - Jesus is our example of self-discipline.
   - Learning to parent by grace is like learning to ride a bicycle.
   - Parenting by grace is a way of life.
4. Write the following five principles of discipline on strips of adding-machine tape: (1) Encourage a child's feelings of self-worth and self-esteem. (2) Guide children toward self-discipline and self-control. (3) Teach a child to relate appropriately to others. (4) Help a child grow toward emotional maturity. (5) Help a child grow toward his or her potential in spiritual and moral development.

During the Session

1. Give an opportunity for members to share prayer requests. Lead in prayer.

DEBRIEFING

2. Briefly review lesson 3, using "Summary" on page 42 in the *Parent's Guide.*
3. Lead a discussion of the activity members completed in "Looking Ahead" on page 42 in the *Parent's Guide.* Ask these questions:
   - What situation did you observe in which your child's behavior depended on discipline from outside sources?
   - What effect did the outside discipline have on your child?
   - What situation did you observe in which your child demonstrated self-discipline?
   - What factors contributed to your child's self-discipline in that situation?

PRESENTATION

4. State the learning goals for this session.
5. Distribute copies of worksheet 15. After members have completed it, involve them in discussing the statements. (See the suggestions for this type of activity in session 3.) Here are our responses to the statements: 1. D. This one is tricky. We don't always know what God's purpose is for our children. We should be very careful and sensitive not to force our children in certain directions. At the same time, we should take a strong role in helping our children discover God's purpose for their lives. 2. D. This one is

also tricky. Of course, it depends on the kind of discipline and the person administering it. But discipline from an outside source is not harmful just because it is external. 3. A. 4. D. The purpose of external discipline is to develop and encourage self-discipline. 5. D. 6. A. 7. A. 8. A. 9. D. Although it is true that parental mistakes can have a detrimental effect on children, our children learn even by how we handle our mistakes. 10. A. 11. A. Although some parents fail to discipline their children, discipline is not optional for any parent. God expects it of us. 12. A. 13. A. 14. D. Parents in the home have the primary responsibility.

6. Refer to the teaching posters on the walls. Ask volunteers to read and comment on the meanings of the signs as a summary of the lesson.
7. Refer to the Bible passages beginning on page 45 in the *Parent's Guide.* Ask volunteers to share the summaries they wrote.
8. Refer to "Checkpoint," beginning on page 49 in the *Parent's Guide.* Ask volunteers to respond to the activities.

SKILL DEVELOPMENT

9. Form four small groups and give each group one of the case studies. Allow a few minutes for small-group work and call for reports.
10. Mount on the chalkboard the strips listing the five principles of discipline. Involve members in discussing their children's relationship to the principles in the areas of self-worth, self-discipline, relationships, emotional maturity, and spiritual and moral development. Ask members to share times when they have practiced and violated these principles. Conclude this activity by asking members to reflect on the following questions.
    - Does my behavior toward my child encourage her self-esteem?
    - Does my method of discipline offer guidance, or is it merely punishment?
    - Does my lifestyle reflect a love for others?
    - Do my actions and reactions to people and situations demonstrate the fruit of the Spirit in my life?
    - Do my actions and attitudes help my child grow in his relationship with Christ?
11. Distribute copies of worksheet 16. Lead in a discussion of
    - the cause(s) of behavior;
    - the influence of the discipline on the child's development;
    - how members would have handled the situations if the discipline is inappropriate.

    Then refer to the situations beginning on page 47 in the *Parent's Guide* and discuss any of them that are of particular interest to the group.
12. Use the chart on page 48 in the *Parent's Guide* to move to a discussion of behavioral problems or patterns in members' children. Refer to the three situations on pages 48–49 and ask members to share how they responded. Then ask members to share recent situations from their own experiences and how they handled them.
13. Refer to the two charts on affirmation and celebration and on discipline and guidance, page 50 in the *Parent's Guide.* Ask members to share in pairs their experiences in these two areas during the past week.
14. Ask members to check their "report cards" in "Reflection and Application" on page 50 in the *Parent's Guide* and to share ways they can improve.
15. If time permits, conclude by asking members to respond in pairs to the questions in activity 7 on page 51 in the *Parent's Guide.*

PREVIEW AND ASSIGNMENT

16. Preview lesson 5 by using the outline poster.
17. Ask members to complete at home the activities in "Looking Ahead" on page 51 in the *Parent's Guide.*

After the Session

Refer to "After the Session" on page 26 in this guide.

WORKSHEET 15

Read each statement. If you agree with the statement, write *A* in the blank. If you disagree with the statement, write *D.* If you are undecided, write *U.*

___ 1. Parents should not take a strong role in determining what God's purpose is for their children.

___ 2. Discipline imposed by another person is harmful to a child's development.

___ 3. Self-discipline is of greater value than discipline from the outside.

___ 4. Discipline from the outside works against and discourages self-discipline.

___ 5. The principles found in the Bible do not speak to many issues of modern life.

___ 6. A good way for parents to teach self-discipline is to demonstrate it in their lives.

___ 7. Unconditional love and discipline are not contradictory.

___ 8. Understanding the cause of a child's behavior is necessary for effective discipline.

___ 9. Mistakes by parents have a detrimental effect on children.

___ 10. Parenting by grace is a lifestyle more than a set of guidelines.

___ 11. Discipline is not optional for a parent.

___ 12. A parent's attitude and actions communicate love to a child better than words.

___ 13. When a parent disciplines a child, it is important to help maintain the child's self-esteem.

___ 14. The church has the primary responsibility for the spiritual development of children.

WORKSHEET 16

Read the following situations. Suggest the probable cause(s) of the child's behavior. How does the parental discipline indicated influence the child's development, especially spiritually and morally?

Situation	Cause(s) of Behavior	Influence of the Discipline on Development
1. Dad constantly argues with 14-year-old Rick about the way he spends his allowance.		
2. Mom and Dad tell 16-year-old Karen, "We appreciate the way you limit your phone calls to 15 or 20 minutes."		
3. Mom fusses at 13-year-old Nancy about her room: "You live like a slob. You know better. You're just lazy."		
4. Dad helps 17-year-old Chad study for an honors history test.		
5. Mom and Dad agree to let 15-year-old Mike go to an after-the-game party if he refuses to drink alcoholic beverages or use drugs.		
6. Mom and Dad ground 15-year-old Steve for two weeks because he stormed out of the room and slammed his bedroom door in anger at a decision his parents made for him.		

Case Study 3

Analyze the following case study.

The Petersens have cable television in their home. Late at night several channels broadcast R-rated and X-rated movies. Kim, 14, often stays up until two or three o'clock in the morning watching these movies. Her parents are fully aware of what she's doing, but they figure she's old enough to make her own decisions about what she watches.

1. Does this situation describe discipline from outside, self-discipline, or no discipline?

   ____

2. If you were the parent, how would you respond to the situation? If needed, how could discipline by grace be applied?

   ____

   ____

Case Study 4

Analyze the following case study.

Beth is overweight. Her mother takes her to a weight-reduction clinic, where a trainer recommends that Beth begin exercising. Beth hates to exercise. Her mother takes her to an exercise class every Monday, Wednesday, Friday, and Saturday. She goes to the class, too, just to make sure that Beth participates.

1. Does this situation describe discipline from outside, self-discipline, or no discipline?

   ____

2. If you were the parent, how would you respond to the situation? If needed, how could discipline by grace be applied?

   ____

   ____

Case Study 5

Analyze the following case study.

Keith's parents bought him a motorcycle. He drives it around the neighborhood, through people's yards, even across the front lawn of the church while worship is in session. He drives fast and recklessly. Some of the neighbors have called his parents, asking them to do something about it. They just laugh, saying, "Oh, you know how boys are!"

1. Does this situation describe discipline from outside, self-discipline, or no discipline?

   ____

2. If you were the parent, how would you respond to the situation? If needed, how could discipline by grace be applied?

   ____

   ____

Case Study 6

Analyze the following case study.

Reagan has to read three books during summer vacation. When she returns to school in the fall, she'll be required to take a test on each book. Reagan doesn't enjoy reading, especially "this boring stuff," as she refers to it. Her mother is sympathetic, but she insists that Reagan read at least one chapter each day before she goes to the swim club with her friends.

1. Does this situation describe discipline from outside, self-discipline, or no discipline?

   ____

2. If you were the parent, how would you respond to the situation? If needed, how could discipline by grace be applied?

   ____

   ____

UNIT 3

How to Discipline by Grace

Session 5

Discipline Affirms Appropriate Behavior

Session Goals

After completing this session, members should better understand how to use discipline to affirm appropriate behavior. They will be able to

- define *appropriate behavior* and name three factors on which appropriate behavior depends;
- state at least five methods of reinforcing appropriate behavior;
- identify and reinforce at least three appropriate behaviors in their children this week.

Before the Session

1. Carefully study lesson 5 and complete all of the learning activities.
2. Duplicate worksheets 17 and 18 and case studies 7 and 8.
3. Write the following statements on large sheets of newsprint. Mount the sheets in random order on the walls around the room.
   - Parents model their interpretations of appropriate behavior.
   - Children learn from models.
   - Punishment that tears down a child's spirit has no place in a home.
   - The basic tools of discipline by grace are affirmation and encouragement.
   - The spiritual development of children depends on parents who affirm appropriate behavior.
   - Discipline focuses on the future.
   - Punishment focuses on the past.
   - Children need to feel the consequences of what they do.
   - Often we expect children to be more controlled than we are.
   - Specific compliments mean more.

During the Session

1. Distribute copies of worksheet 17 as members arrive and ask them to complete it before the session begins.
2. Welcome members. Share prayer requests and lead in prayer.

DEBRIEFING

3. Review lesson 4, using "Summary" on page 51 in the *Parent's Guide.*
4. Ask members to share with a partner the activities they completed in "Looking Ahead" in lesson 4, page 51 in the *Parent's Guide.*

PRESENTATION

5. Call attention to the learning goals for the session.
6. Lead in a discussion of worksheet 17 as answers are shared. This worksheet covers the entire lesson. Answers: 1. T; 2. T, 3. F, 4. F; 5. T, 6. F, 7. F, 8. T, 9. F, 10. T, 11. T, 12. F. This one is tricky. It is true that parents should be consistent. But acknowledging unique characteristics of children may be interpreted as having different definitions of appropriate behavior for each child (see p. 55 in the *Parent's Guide*). 13. F, 14. F, 15. T, 16. T, 17. T, 18. F. The heart of parenting by grace is unconditional love.
7. Refer to the agree/disagree activity on page 53 in the *Parent's Guide.* Involve members in a discussion of the statements. Write this question on the chalk-

board: *Should appropriate behavior be defined differently for girls and boys?* Discuss responses.

8. Ask volunteers to read aloud the teaching posters and to comment on their meanings.
9. Refer to "Checkpoint" on page 58 in the *Parent's Guide.* Ask volunteers to share their work.

SKILL DEVELOPMENT

10. Refer to members' evaluations of how well they practice the methods of affirming appropriate behavior (p. 59 in the *Parent's Guide*). Ask members to select the one method they practice best and the one method on which they need the most improvement.
11. Distribute copies of worksheet 18. Ask members to share their responses in pairs.
12. Refer to worksheet 8, the personality profile given out in session 1. Relate it to the importance of reinforcing each child's unique personality. Also review the activities in "Looking Ahead" on page 51 in the *Parent's Guide.*
13. Divide members into two or more small groups and distribute case studies 7 and 8. (If you have more than two small groups, use the same case study with different groups.)
14. Ask members to share in pairs their experiences in identifying and reinforcing appropriate behavior during the past week (activity 1 in "Reflection and Application," p. 58 in the *Parent's Guide*).
15. While members are still in pairs, ask them to respond to the remaining questions in "Reflection and Application."
16. Announce that the group is halfway through the course. Spend a few minutes evaluating the course and the group process by asking the questions in activity 4 of "Reflection and Application" on page 59 in the *Parent's Guide.*

PREVIEW AND ASSIGNMENT

17. Preview lesson 6 by using the outline poster.
18. Ask members to complete at home the activity in "Looking Ahead" on page 59 in the *Parent's Guide.*
19. Close with prayer.

After the Session

Refer to "After the Session" on page 26 in this guide.

WORKSHEET 17

Mark each statement *T* (true) or *F* (false).

___ 1. Appropriate behavior depends on the developmental level of the child.
___ 2. Having consistent expectations is a key principle of discipline.
___ 3. Specific circumstances should not redefine appropriate behavior.
___ 4. Children who are encouraged for keeping rules instead of punished for breaking them do not learn self-discipline.
___ 5. Children who receive punishment as the main source of discipline do not resist temptation as well as children who are encouraged and praised.
___ 6. Discipline by grace does not include rebuke.
___ 7. Parents should hold the same expectations of appropriate behavior for all of their children.
___ 8. Affirmation and encouragement are important parts of discipline.
___ 9. Discipline should always be positive.
___ 10. Affirmation and encouragement should match the child's age.
___ 11. A child's feelings as well as behavior should be reinforced.
___ 12. Parents should consistently treat all of their children the same.
___ 13. General compliments reinforce better than specific compliments.
___ 14. It is not possible to praise a child too much.
___ 15. A child can become overly dependent on praise from others.
___ 16. External praise could cause a child to be more vulnerable to inappropriate suggestions or directives from others.
___ 17. A parent's response to his child's friends is an indirect response to the parent's child.
___ 18. Sometimes a parent's conditional love for a child is appropriate.

WORKSHEET 18

Complete this worksheet. Then share your responses with another group member.

1. Describe an incident when you purposefully scouted ahead to avoid placing your child in a situation he was not mature enough to handle.

____

____

2. Describe a time when you unwittingly put your child in a situation that automatically led to misbehavior.

____

____

3. What were your feelings? How did you handle the situation?

____

____

4. What specific steps could you have taken to avoid the problem?

____

____

5. Review your child's behavior this past week. Name some things he or she did that made you feel good.

____

____

6. How could you have praised your child specifically for these appropriate behaviors?

____

____

7. If you have used specific praise in the past for encouraging good behavior, what effect did it have on future behavior?

____

____

Case Study 7

Analyze the following case study.

It has been a difficult, tiring day. Your patience is depleted, and you are abrupt with everyone. Supper is finally over, and the kitchen is straight again. Exhausted, you slump into your favorite chair, thinking only of a few minutes of peace and quiet. Immediately, your three-year-old crawls into your lap and says: "Play with me, please. Play with me."

1. What is your first reaction?

2. How would you respond?

3. Which methods of affirming appropriate behavior could be used in this situation?

Case Study 8

Analyze the following case study.

Seventeen-year-old Barb just came in 30 minutes late from a date because she and her boyfriend had a fight. Dad says: "I know you're upset, but you know the rules. You're grounded for a week. I'm sorry things are rotten for you right now." Barb screams: "Sorry, huh? You don't care about anything but your old rules. I hate you!" She runs to her room and slams the door. Dad yells after her: "I will not allow that kind of display of emotion in this house. You're grounded for two weeks!"

1. Do you agree with the father's response? Explain.

2. How would you have handled the situation?

3. Which methods of affirming appropriate behavior could be used in this situation?

Session 6

Discipline Finds Alternatives to Replace Inappropriate Behavior

Session Goals

After completing this session, members should better understand how to handle inappropriate behavior. They will be able to

- define *inappropriate behavior;*
- state two results or consequences of a parent's focusing on inappropriate behavior but failing to handle it properly;
- state at least five methods for dealing with inappropriate behavior;
- analyze at least one behavioral pattern with their children in which the behavior is inappropriate and outline plans for dealing with the situation;
- implement at least three methods for dealing with inappropriate behavior.

Before the Session

1. Carefully study lesson 6 and complete all of the learning activities. You may want to call members to check on their progress in the course.
2. Duplicate worksheets 19, 20, and 21 and case studies 9, 10, and 11.
3. Write the following statements on large sheets of newsprint. Mount the sheets in random order on the walls around the room.
   - A negative atmosphere in a home hurts a child.
   - Children who are often discouraged are more likely to be aggressive.
   - The balance of discipline needs to be on the side of reinforcement.
   - Children need to feel our unconditional love, even when we are angry.
   - Simple solutions to complex problems are difficult to find.
   - Children need to learn from their mistakes.
   - Children need to know what the boundaries are.
   - Boundaries need to give a child room to grow.
   - Children often turn out to look and act like their parents!
   - Don't expect from your children what you aren't willing to do.
   - Do not punish a child for something he cannot yet understand.
   - Put yourself in your child's place.
   - Use an arrow, not a shotgun.
   - The parent who yells all the time is soon ignored.
   - Don't decide on the discipline when you're angry.

During the Session

1. Distribute copies of worksheet 19 as members arrive and ask them to begin work on it.
2. Devote the prayer time to family needs. Ask members to cluster in small groups, to share prayer requests, and to pray.

DEBRIEFING

3. Review lesson 5 by asking volunteers to respond to the activities in "Checkpoint" on page 58 in the *Parent's Guide.*
4. Involve members in a discussion of the activity they completed in "Looking Ahead" in lesson 5, page 59 in the *Parent's Guide.* Ask these questions:
   - What did you discover about your response(s) to your child's inappropriate behavior or misbehavior?
   - What is your child learning from your response to his inappropriate behavior?
   - Did logical and natural consequences or artificial and contrived consequences seem more effective in disciplining your child?
   - What appear to be the long-term results of a dependency on artificial and/or contrived consequences?

PRESENTATION

5. Call attention to the learning goals for the session.
6. Call for responses to worksheet 19 and discuss what you consider to be the key points. Answers: 1. threat, 2. bribe, 3. natural, 4. contrived, 5. example, 6. unconditional, 7. understanding, 8. aggressive, 9. behavior, 10. negative, 11. logical, 12. consequences, 13. selective, 14. appropriate, 15. boundaries.
7. Distribute copies of worksheet 20 and allow a few minutes for completion. Involve members in discussing the statements. Here are our responses: 1. A, 2. D, 3. A, 4. D. This one is tricky. It is good to let children experience the natural consequences of their misbehavior in many situations. However, in other situations it is not a good idea. For example, the natural consequences of playing with a gun could be tragic. 5. A. Of course, at certain times and in cer-

tain situations the child cannot be involved. 6. A, 7. D. Of course, parents do some things children cannot do. But for the most part, parents should live by their own boundaries. 8. A, 9. D, 10. D, 11. A.

8. Ask each member to select a teaching poster, to read it to the group, and to comment on its meaning. Allow time for discussion.
9. Ask members to share their work in "Checkpoint" on page 65 in the *Parent's Guide.*

SKILL DEVELOPMENT

10. Refer to the activities on the parent's emphasis in discipline, before beginning this course and at present, and on the atmosphere of the home (p. 61 in the *Parent's Guide*). Ask volunteers to compare their teenagers' perceptions of the home atmosphere with their own ratings. Ask, What can be learned from this? Allow time for discussion.
11. Refer to the "report card" on methods for dealing with inappropriate behavior (activity 3, "Reflection and Application," p. 66 in the *Parent's Guide*). Ask members to share areas in which they need to improve.
12. Refer to the activities on boundaries on page 63 in the *Parent's Guide.* Ask members to share their responses with partners.
13. Distribute copies of worksheet 21. Allow a few minutes for completion. Ask members to share several responses. Then read to the group the following reasons for the behavior as you discuss the situations one at a time. Ask: Does this additional information make any difference in how you would discipline the child? How would it change your method or degree of discipline?
    - Tammy wanted to help her father with his cleaning chores. In dusting his table, she knocked off his clock radio.
    - Anne borrowed her mother's money to buy a Bible for a friend who had just expressed an interest in becoming a Christian.
    - On the way to school, Mike saw a dog get run over by a hit-and-run driver. The dog was badly injured. He took it to the vet.
    - Leigh took a casserole to the family of a friend whose mother was in the hospital.
14. Divide members into three small groups according to the ages of their children (preschool, elementary-age, teenager). Form more than one small group per age group if needed. Assign case study 9 to parents of preschoolers, case study 10 to parents of elementary-age children, and case study 11 to parents of teenagers. Allow a few minutes for small-group work and call for reports.
15. Ask the small groups to discuss activities 1 and 2 in "Reflection and Application," beginning on page 65 in the *Parent's Guide.*
16. If time permits, refer to the teaching posters and spend a few minutes discussing them.

PREVIEW AND ASSIGNMENT

17. Preview lesson 7 by using the outline poster.
18. Ask members to complete at home the activities in "Looking Ahead" on page 67 in the *Parent's Guide.*
19. Close with prayer.

After the Session

Refer to "After the Session" on page 26 in this guide.

WORKSHEET 19

Refer to lesson 6 as needed to complete the crossword puzzle.

15
9
12
7
13
10
1
3
11
5
2
6
14
4
8

Across

1. This type of discipline has negative side effects.
2. An inappropriate method of discipline.
3. Consequences children experience as a direct result of their behavior.
4. Consequences imposed by the parent unrelated to the problem behavior.
5. Children view their parents in this role.
6. A mark of parental love in parenting by grace.
7. A parent should get this from the child's point of view before disciplining the child.
8. This nature develops in children when they do not have suitable alternatives to inappropriate behavior.
9. This should be labeled rather than the child.

Down

10. The resulting atmosphere in the home when a child's misbehavior and an ineffective parental response dominate the family relationship.
11. Consequences imposed by the parent related to the problem behavior.
12. When children misbehave, they need to feel these.
13. A parent should be this way in responding to a child's misbehavior.
14. This kind of behavior must be emphasized when dealing with misbehavior.
15. It is important that these be set in advance.

WORKSHEET 20

Read each statement. If you agree with the statement, write *A* in the blank. If you disagree with the statement, write *D.* If you are undecided, write *U.*

___ 1. A parent should focus on affirming appropriate behavior.

___ 2. Inappropriate behavior, as a rule, should be ignored.

___ 3. Physical punishment usually teaches a child the wrong thing.

___ 4. Children should be protected from the consequences of their misbehavior.

___ 5. Children should be involved in helping to set boundaries and rules.

___ 6. Each boundary should have a purpose.

___ 7. Parents should not be expected to abide by the same rules they have set for their children.

___ 8. Spanking is not an effective means of discipline.

___ 9. Discipline should not follow misbehavior immediately.

___ 10. Contrived consequences for misbehavior are more effective than natural consequences.

___ 11. Consequences should relate to the problem behavior as much as possible.

WORKSHEET 21

Read the following descriptions of behaviors. How would you react if your child acted this way, based only on surface facts?

1. Five-year-old Tammy knocked her father's clock radio off the bedside table and broke it.

____

____

____

2. Fourteen-year-old Anne and her mother were in the checkout line at the grocery store. Mom reached into her purse to pay her bill, and her money was missing. Anne said: "Oh, Mom! I forgot! I borrowed your money!"

____

____

____

3. Eleven-year-old Mike was two hours late to school. The principal called his father to report that Mike didn't have an excuse.

____

____

____

4. The casserole Leigh's mother was planning to have for supper was not in the freezer when she looked for it. "Do you know anything about this, Leigh?"

   "Yes," Leigh answered. "I took it out."

   "I've told you not to prepare food I'm saving for something else," her mother said angrily.

____

____

____

Case Study 9

Read the following situations in which a parent tries to correct a child's inappropriate behavior.

- Decide whether the parent's behavior is acceptable or unacceptable.
- In each situation what is the child being taught by the parent's response?
- What are likely to be the long-term consequences of the parental response?
- If the parent's behavior is unacceptable, what did he or she do wrong?
- How would you have handled the situation?

1. Meghan, age two, has just spilled her apple juice for the third time this morning. Her mother grabs the cup from her, slaps her hand, and yells: "You're such a clumsy child! You'll not have any more juice until you can hold it and not spill it."
2. Five-year-old Andrew refuses to go to bed at bedtime. He cries, gets out of bed, and even kicks and hits when his father carries him, screaming, to his room. The fourth time his dad just gives in and lets him stay up, but he says coldly: "I don't care what you do, Andrew. Stay up all night if you want to. But I'm going to remember this the next time you want me to do anything for you."

Case Study 10

Read the following situations in which a parent tries to correct a child's inappropriate behavior.

- Decide whether the parent's behavior is acceptable or unacceptable.
- In each situation what is the child being taught by the parent's response?
- What are likely to be the long-term consequences of the parental response?
- If the parent's behavior is unacceptable, what did he or she do wrong?
- How would you have handled the situation?

1. Jonathan, eight, is on vacation with his parents. They've been riding in the car for about eight hours with only three or four stops. He's cranky and hyperactive. When they finally arrive at the motel, he wants to go swimming. His mother says, "We're going to eat dinner; then we're going to ride downtown and see the sights." Jonathan starts crying and says, "I want to go swimming!" They argue back and forth for about 15 minutes. Finally, Jonathan's father says: "You're not going anywhere but to bed! We can't take you anywhere!"
2. Marcy is a sixth-grader. She has never understood math well and is afraid of her math teacher. One day Marcy decides to skip class and hides in the girls' restroom. Mrs. Dodd, her teacher, discovers her and calls her mother. Marcy's mother is furious. She drives to the school and starts shouting at Marcy in front of her teacher: "Marcy, I can't believe you'd do a thing like this! What an embarrassment! You're going to end up flunking out of school and disgracing the family!" Marcy begins to cry. She tries to explain why, but her mother stops her: "There's no excuse for this. Wait and see what your father says! No more television! No more new clothes! No more spending the night with friends! You're in big trouble!"

Case Study 11

Read the following situations in which a parent tries to correct a child's inappropriate behavior.

- Decide whether the parent's behavior is acceptable or unacceptable.
- In each situation what is the child being taught by the parent's response?
- What are likely to be the long-term consequences of the parental response?
- If the parent's behavior is unacceptable, what did he or she do wrong?
- How would you have handled the situation?

1. Dale, 14, is on vacation with her parents. One day at the motel swimming pool, she meets several other teenagers. They ask her to go with them to a hamburger place down the beach. Dale's parents are in the motel room. She decides to go without asking them first and is gone for about 2½ hours. When she gets back, her parents are frantic with worry. Her father asks her why she didn't tell them where she was going. "I don't know, Dad. I guess I just forgot." He answers: "Dale, you know how much your mother and I love you. When you disappear like that, it causes us all kinds of anxiety. Do you think that's fair?" "No, Dad." He puts his arms around her shoulders. "We want you to make friends, Sweetheart, but we also want to know where you are, especially when we're out of town and you're with people we don't know. From now on, please keep us posted."
2. Both of Brandon's parents are professional musicians. Brandon has been taking piano lessons since he was 6. At 15, he's beginning to develop other interests, especially tennis. He's not particularly gifted in music, even though his parents require him to practice for an hour every day. One afternoon his tennis coach invites him to play in a prestigious tournament with a rival school. There's only one problem: it's on the same day as his piano lesson. Brandon decides not to tell his parents about the conflict but leads them to believe that he's going to his piano lesson, when he really plans to play in the tournament. When he doesn't show up for the lesson, his teacher calls his parents. His mother is furious. When Brandon tries to explain, she cuts him off: "You are the most ungrateful child I've ever seen. Throwing away nine years of lessons for nothing! No more tennis. If you can't set your priorities, I'll set them for you!"

UNIT 4

Applying Grace to Your Parenting

Session 7

Seizing the Teachable Moment

Session Goals

After completing this session, members should better understand how to use the teachable moment in the parenting process. They will be able to

- define *teachable moment;*
- describe their responsibilities as teachers in parenting;
- state at least four guidelines for recognizing and using teachable moments;
- structure an opportunity for a teachable moment with their children;
- evaluate a teachable-moment experience with their children.

Before the Session

1. Carefully study lesson 7 and complete all of the learning activities.
2. Duplicate case studies 12, 13, 14, 15, 16, and 17.
3. Write the following statements on large sheets of newsprint. Mount the sheets in random order on the walls around the room.
   - Values and beliefs are more easily caught than taught.
   - One-to-one instruction is a superior method of teaching.
   - Teachable moments are daily opportunities to guide our children toward Christian maturity.
   - Parents are to be teachers, not smoke detectors.
   - Special moments come in everyday life to teach our children spiritual and moral values.
   - Teachable moments make lasting impressions on children.
   - Children are not miniature adults.
   - Put yourself in your child's shoes.
   - Ask a question; then count to 20.
   - It's OK to say, "I don't know."
   - Little things count a lot.
   - If you do not take time to mend your child's broken toy, she will never come to you for help in mending a broken heart.
   - We can create teachable moments.
   - Our child is God's child.

During the Session

1. Welcome members. Ask for prayer requests and call on someone to lead in prayer.

DEBRIEFING

2. Review lesson 6, using "Checkpoint" on page 65 in the *Parent's Guide.* Ask for volunteers to share answers to the activities as members check their work.
3. Allow ample time for members to share and discuss any experiences they have had applying what they have learned in any previous session. Suggest the following topics to get the group started:
   - Increasing or decreasing the number of "I" messages and "you" messages given
   - The amount of time spent with children
   - The use of affirmation and celebration of behavior
   - Reinforcing appropriate behavior
   - Handling inappropriate behavior
4. Involve members in discussing the activities they completed in "Looking Ahead" in lesson 6, page 67 in the *Parent's Guide.* Ask these questions:

- What words did you use to describe the most influential teacher (other than your parents) in your life?
- How did this person use teachable moments?
- What are some teachable moments you remember from your childhood?
- Were your parents available to you in everyday events?
- What factors contributed to a teachable moment you experienced with your parents?
- How can you become more sensitive to spontaneous teachable moments with your child?

PRESENTATION

5. Call attention to the learning goals for the session.
6. Ask for examples of how Jesus used teachable moments. (You may wish to refer to activity 4 in "Reflection and Application" on p. 74 in the *Parent's Guide.*)
7. Referring to the true/false activity beginning on page 69 in the *Parent's Guide,* discuss the statements as answers are shared. (Answers begin on p. 72.)
8. Ask each member to select a teaching poster, to read it to the group, and to comment on its meaning.
9. Refer to "Checkpoint" on page 73 in the *Parent's Guide.* Ask members to check their work as answers are shared.
10. Emphasize the importance of parents' example and teaching. Use the examples of Bible parents and their children (see the chart on p. 70 in the *Parent's Guide*).

SKILL DEVELOPMENT

11. Refer to the "report card" on using the guidelines for teachable moments (activity 3, "Reflection and Application," p. 73 in the *Parent's Guide*). Ask members to share in pairs the guidelines on which they scored lowest.
12. Refer to the situations in "Responding to Teachable Moments" on page 73 in the *Parent's Guide.* Call for volunteers to share their responses.
13. Form three or more small groups by the ages of members' children (preschool, elementary-age, teenagers). Assign case studies 12 (preschool), 13 (elementary-age), and 14 (teenager). Allow a few minutes for small-group work and call for reports.
14. Assign the same small groups case studies 15 (preschool), 16 (elementary-age), and 17 (teenagers). Allow a few minutes for small-group work and call for reports.
15. Ask members to share their experiences with teachable moments during the past week. Refer to activities 1 and 2 in "Reflection and Application," page 73 in the *Parent's Guide.* Also refer to the teachable-moment chart (activity 6 on p. 74).
16. Lead the group in discussing the following questions.
    - Do you find it difficult or easy to talk with your child about spiritual matters?
    - If your 10-year-old came to you and said, "I want to become a Christian," what would you do? How would you help your child?
17. Call for reports on members' experiences reinforcing appropriate behavior and dealing with misbehavior. Refer to the charts in activities 7 and 8 on page 74 in the *Parent's Guide.*

PREVIEW AND ASSIGNMENT

18. Preview lesson 8 by using the outline poster.
19. Ask members to complete at home the activity in "Looking Ahead" on page 75 in the *Parent's Guide.*
20. Close with prayer.

After the Session

Refer to "After the Session" on page 26 in this guide.

Case Study 12

Analyze the following behaviors of parents toward their children.

- Do you agree with the parent's behavior?
- Decide whether the parent is recognizing and using teachable moments.
- If the parent is not using teachable moments, what actions could be taken to do so?

1. Sarah is three years old. Her mother takes her grocery shopping with her but makes her sit very still in the shopping cart.
2. Alex is six months old. Sometimes his mother shakes him and gives him a spanking when he won't stop crying.

Case Study 13

Analyze the following behaviors of parents toward their children.

- Do you agree with the parent's behavior?
- Decide whether the parent is recognizing and using teachable moments.
- If the parent is not using teachable moments, what actions could be taken to do so?

1. Mr. Brown won't allow his 11-year-old daughter to go to the three-day state-camp assembly for GA girls because "She's never been away from home before, and she might get homesick."
2. Steve, 9, has a weekly allowance for church, school lunches, school supplies, and spending money.

Case Study 14

Analyze the following behaviors of parents toward their children.

- Do you agree with the parent's behavior?
- Decide whether the parent is recognizing and using teachable moments.
- If the parent is not using teachable moments, what actions could be taken to do so?

1. Because Andrea is 13, her parents told her she doesn't need to consult them anymore about what classes to take each year in school. She's old enough now to plan her own schedule.
2. Greg, 15, has been visiting a church of a denomination different from his parents'. He wants to become a member, but his parents won't allow him to join the other church until he's 18.

Case Study 15

Read the following situations in which children are misbehaving.

- Think of a specific solution for each misbehavior.
- How could the parent discipline by encouragement instead of punishment?
- What opportunity does the parent have to teach in each situation?
- Could any of the situations be turned into teachable moments?

1. Every afternoon sets the stage for a battle of wills between Lindsey and her mother. Exhausted, Lindsey fusses and refuses to take a nap unless her mother lies down with her.
2. Tara and her daddy are at the grocery store. Tara won't sit in the cart. She wants to walk by herself, but she keeps pulling things off the shelf and putting them in the basket.

Case Study 16

Read the following situations in which children are misbehaving.

- Think of a specific solution for each misbehavior.
- How could the parent discipline by encouragement instead of punishment?
- What opportunity does the parent have to teach in each situation?
- Could any of the situations be turned into teachable moments?

1. Eleven-year-old Debbie and her father are at the shopping mall. Debbie begs to stop at every store to look at the cosmetics, even though she knows that her father is in a hurry to finish his errands and go home.
2. Philip and Craig, both 10, want to sit together in church; but every time they do, they giggle and whisper.

Case Study 17

Read the following situations in which children are misbehaving.

- Think of a specific solution for each misbehavior.
- How could the parent discipline by encouragement instead of punishment?
- What opportunity does the parent have to teach in each situation?
- Could any of the situations be turned into teachable moments?

1. The Hendersons take their two teenage sons, Ralph and Bob, to church at 4:00 on Sunday for youth-choir practice. Evening worship doesn't begin until 6:30. The minister of music just told them that Ralph and Bob haven't been to youth choir in two consecutive weeks.
2. Tina, a bright 17-year-old, has started cutting her French class. She says that she's bored and that her teacher can't speak French as well as she can.

Session 8

Teaching Through Example

Session Goals

After completing this session, members should better understand teaching through example. They will be able to

- define *modeling* as a parenting technique;
- state at least four guidelines for teaching through example;
- identify two of their limitations as models;
- name the three primary models in children's lives;
- take at least two specific actions to become better models in their parenting.

Before the Session

1. Carefully study lesson 8 and complete all of the learning activities.
2. Duplicate worksheets 22 and 23.
3. Write the following statements on large sheets of newsprint. Mount the sheets in random order on the walls around the room.
   - We are examples our children strive to equal or excel.
   - Our behavior teaches more powerfully than any other way of teaching.
   - Modeling is the greatest way to help children grow spiritually and morally.
   - Values are the beliefs and involvements to which we give our time, money, and energy.
   - We continually choose what we will invest ourselves in.
   - We teach love when we show love.
   - Children learn to trust Jesus by first learning to trust us.
   - God chose us to help Him work out His purpose for His creation.
   - No one is an object to be used.
   - Children learn by doing.
   - I'm sorry.
   - Children are confronted with a host of conflicting models.

During the Session

1. Distribute copies of worksheet 22 as members arrive and ask them to begin work on it.
2. Call for sharing and prayer requests. Lead in prayer.

DEBRIEFING

3. Review lesson 7, using "Checkpoint" on page 73 in the *Parent's Guide.* Ask volunteers to share their answers as members check their work.
4. Allow time for members to share and discuss any experiences they have had applying what they have learned in the course.
5. Involve members in discussing the influential model, other than their parents, in their lives. See "Looking Ahead" on page 75 in the *Parent's Guide.* Ask these questions:
   - Whom did you select and why?
   - What learning experiences come to mind as you think of this person?
   - Does this person know that he or she has been a model for your life?

PRESENTATION

6. Call attention to the learning goals for the session.
7. Involve members in a discussion of worksheet 22. Here are our responses: 1. D. Although it is difficult for a child to overcome the influence of a negative parental model, in God's providence it is possible for a person to overcome such an influence. 2. A. 3. A. 4. D. This one is tricky. As a rule, our behavior should be consistent with our expectations for our children. However, the world always changes the meaning of the statement. In certain areas, such as driving the car, the parent's behavior is not consistent with his expectations for his child. 5. A. 6. A. 7. A. 8. D. 9. D. This one is ambiguous. Much television programming provides a detrimental model for children, but certainly all television is not in that category. 10. D. 11. D. It is very important for the child to have other adult models.
8. Refer to "Checkpoint" on page 81 in the *Parent's Guide.* Ask members to check their work as volunteers share their responses.
9. Ask each member to select a teaching poster, to read it to the group, and to comment on its meaning.

SKILL DEVELOPMENT

10. Refer to the "report card" on using the guidelines for teaching through example (activity 3, "Reflection and Application," p. 81 in the *Parent's Guide*). Ask members to share in pairs the guidelines on which they scored lowest.

11. Refer to the list of priority values on page 77 in the *Parent's Guide.* Involve members in discussing the questions related to these values on page 78.
12. Refer to the chart on page 78 comparing expectations for the child with the parent's behavior. Ask members to name areas in which they need to improve.
13. Briefly review the activity on unspoken needs (activity 4) on page 79 in the *Parent's Guide.* Lead in a discussion of members' responses. Distribute copies of worksheet 23 and ask members to complete it in pairs. Allow a few minutes for group work and then lead in a sharing-and-discussion time on the activity.
14. Write on the chalkboard: *Three Primary Models in Children's Lives.* List under this heading the words *Parents, Television,* and *Peer Groups.* Refer to the chart "Parental Response to Television" on page 80 in the *Parent's Guide.* Lead members in discussing the activity.
15. Lead members in discussing the activity on teachable moments on page 82 in the *Parent's Guide.*
16. Refer to the activity on reinforcing appropriate behavior on page 82 in the *Parent's Guide.* Ask members to share their experiences in this area.
17. Ask members to turn to activity 6 in "Reflection and Application" on page 82 in the *Parent's Guide.* Ask them to share in pairs their responses to the questions. Spend a few minutes with the entire group discussing some of the questions.

PREVIEW AND ASSIGNMENT

18. Preview lesson 9 by using the outline poster.
19. Assign the activity in "Looking Ahead" on page 82 in the *Parent's Guide* for members to complete at home.
20. Close with prayer.

After the Session

Refer to "After the Session" on page 26 in this guide.

WORKSHEET 22

Read each statement. If you agree with the statement, write *A* in the blank. If you disagree with the statement, write *D.* If you are undecided, write *U.*

____ 1. A child cannot overcome the influence of a negative parental model.

____ 2. A child senses and knows the values held by a parent.

____ 3. Material possessions should not be a priority in a person's life.

____ 4. A parent's behavior in a certain area should always be consistent with his expectations for the child in that same area.

____ 5. We should treat all persons with respect and consideration.

____ 6. Children often communicate unspoken needs through their questions.

____ 7. Church involvement is essential for one to parent effectively.

____ 8. A parent should not let his child know of his own mistakes.

____ 9. Television is a detrimental model for children.

____ 10. Elementary-age children are more vulnerable to negative peer pressure than teenagers are.

____ 11. Parents should be sure that their child does not have any other adult models.

WORKSHEET 23

The following questions are typical of questions children of various ages ask. State what you think may be the need behind the question. Then think of how you might respond to the spoken question and also meet the unspoken need.

Preschoolers

1. "Do you love me?"

Unspoken need: ____________________

Response: ____________________

2. "Where does God live?"

Unspoken need: ____________________

Response: ____________________

Elementary-Age Children

1. "Whom do you love more, Mommy, me or Daddy?"

Unspoken need: ____________________

Response: ____________________

2. "What is heaven like?"

Unspoken need: ____________________

Response: ____________________

Teenagers

1. "How do I know if I'm really a Christian?"

Unspoken need: ____________________

Response: ____________________

2. "Do you think anyone really loves me?"

Unspoken need: ____________________

Response: ____________________

UNIT 5

Sustaining Grace in Your Parenting

Session 9

Experiencing and Celebrating Family

Session Goals

After completing this session, members should better understand how to experience and celebrate family. They will be able to

- list at least three needs of their family members that can be met through a family time;
- describe Familytime, including its five elements;
- list at least five benefits of Familytime;
- state at least four guidelines for planning for and participating in Familytime;
- analyze their family times;
- commit to begin Familytime and plan to conduct at least four sessions.

Before the Session

1. Carefully study lesson 9 and complete all of the learning activities.
2. Duplicate worksheet 24 and case studies 18, 19, and 20.
3. Write the following statements on large sheets of newsprint. Mount the sheets in random order on the walls around the room.
   - The job of parenting continues throughout life.
   - The job of parenting is continually redefined.
   - Parents continue to model throughout life.
   - Spending time together is an important part of parenting by grace.
   - Familytime focuses on being together and celebrating family.
   - Children need the opportunity to identify and share individual moments worthy of celebration.
   - Sharing grief diminishes the grief; sharing joy enhances the joy.
   - A family needs time away from the routines of housework.
   - Families should play together as well as pray together.
   - Children need to be able to communicate feelings within an understanding family environment.
   - Children appreciate the importance of working and playing together as a family.
   - Familytime activities should be short and simple.
   - The home should have an atmosphere of encouragement and support.
4. Write on strips of adding-machine tape the nine guidelines for planning for and participating in Familytime. Mount the strips on the chalkboard or on the front wall.
   - Keep activities short and simple.
   - Schedule it at children's prime time.
   - Make sure everyone is available.
   - Plan a good snack.
   - Maintain an atmosphere of encouragement and support.
   - Encourage each person to participate in his or her own way.
   - Do not compare work.
   - Encourage children to work at their own pace.
   - Collect materials needed.
5. If you are aware of any group members who already have a regular family time each week, enlist two or three a week in advance to be prepared to give brief testimonies. Ask them to share
   - how long they have been having family times and why they started;
   - how they plan and schedule this time;

- problems associated with planning and scheduling this time;
- how they keep family time from becoming forced and artificial;
- children's response to family time;
- what the parents like least about family time;
- what they like best about family time.

During the Session

1. Distribute copies of worksheet 24 for members to complete as a presession activity.
2. Let the prayer time be a period of thanksgiving for families. Lead the group in sentence prayers.

DEBRIEFING

3. Review lesson 8, using "Checkpoint" on page 81 in the *Parent's Guide.* Ask members to check their work as volunteers share answers.
4. Ask members to share about family celebrations and special events in their childhood. See "Looking Ahead" in lesson 8, page 82 in the *Parent's Guide.* Ask these questions:
   - What were some of the celebrations and special events?
   - What made them special to you?
   - How did you participate as a child in your family celebrations?
   - What elements of the family celebrations were most meaningful to you?
   - What long-term benefit do you think these family times of your childhood have been to you?

PRESENTATION

5. Say, "My family is special because ..." and then finish the sentence in your own words. Lead the entire group in completing the sentence.
6. Call attention to the learning goals for the session.
7. Ask each member to select a teaching poster, to read it to the group, and to comment on its meaning. Allow time for discussion.
8. Refer to worksheet 24 and involve members in discussing the statements. Here are our responses: 1. D. The job of parenting continues throughout the life span. 2. D. 3. A. 4. D. Teenagers may appear not to want to spend time with their families, but they do. 5. A. 6. A. 7. A. 8. D. Familytime is for every member of the family. 9. A. 10. D. The focus should be on encouragement and support. 11. A. 12. D. Discipline is guidance, and much guidance can be given during Familytime. 13. D.
9. Refer to "Checkpoint," beginning on page 87 in the *Parent's Guide.* Ask members to share their work.

SKILL DEVELOPMENT

10. Divide members into small groups according to the ages of their children (preschool, elementary-age, teenagers). Refer to the chart evaluating family time together last week on page 86 in the *Parent's Guide.* Also refer to activity 2 in "Reflection and Application," page 88 in the *Parent's Guide.* Ask the groups to spend a few minutes discussing strengths and weaknesses of their family times.
11. If you have arranged for testimonies, call on the assigned persons to give them.
12. Refer to the sentence strips on guidelines for planning and participating in Familytime. Using the same small groups, distribute case study 18 to parents of preschoolers, case study 19 to parents of elementary-age children, and case study 20 to parents of teenagers. Ask each group to analyze the plans in light of the nine guidelines. Allow a few minutes for small-group work and call for reports. Discuss ways to involve every family member in the different activities.
13. Refer members to the Familytime suggestions on page 87 in the *Parent's Guide.* Ask groups to plan one complete Familytime. Allow time for small-group work and call for reports. Note: This activity is the heart of this session. Be sure to allow ample time for the small-group work and reports.
14. Ask members to share their experiences in getting their families together to discuss Familytime (see activity 4, p. 88 in the *Parent's Guide*). Take time to discuss any problems members may have encountered in committing as a family to participate in at least four sessions of Familytime. Ask members to join hands and to pray as a group for the commitments their families made.

PREVIEW AND ASSIGNMENT

15. Preview lesson 10 by using the outline poster.
16. Assign members to complete at home the activities in "Looking Ahead" on page 89 in the *Parent's Guide.*

After the Session

Refer to "After the Session" on page 26 in this guide.

WORKSHEET 24

Read each statement. If you agree with the statement, write *A* in the blank. If you disagree with the statement, write *D*. If you are undecided, write *U*.

____ 1. The job of parenting continues until a child has reached adulthood.

____ 2. The basic developmental task of a child's first year of life is the development of motor skills.

____ 3. Preschoolers need to develop a healthy sense of autonomy.

____ 4. Teenagers do not want to spend time with their families.

____ 5. Mealtime is an important time for the family to be together.

____ 6. Children should be involved in planning family times together.

____ 7. Every child has accomplishments and moments that should be celebrated by the family.

____ 8. Familytime is primarily for the benefit of young children.

____ 9. A family time together helps create teachable moments.

____ 10. Familytime focuses on sharing problems.

____ 11. Recreation is an important part of Familytime.

____ 12. Discipline should not take place during Familytime.

____ 13. Familytime should last approximately three hours each week.

Case Study 18

Analyze the following plans the Brown family made for a Familytime especially for their preschooler. The Brown family has three children: Wanda, a 4-year-old; Jack, a 9-year-old; and Sue, 14.

- Have the nine guidelines been followed?
- What appear to be the strengths and weaknesses of this plan?

Familytime Plans

Supplies: large sheets of paper, tempera paint, smock or old shirt, bowl, magnifying glass, snack food and drink.

Activity: Begin by telling Wanda a story about her arrival to our family. Let this story convey our love and joy at Wanda's presence in our lives. Begin, "Once upon a time ..." and conclude with "And we are living happily ever after."

Gather a few large sheets of paper and some tempera paint or other water-soluble paint. Put a smock or an old shirt on Wanda to protect her clothes. Pour the paint into a shallow bowl or another container. Let her dip her hand in the paint, then press it, palm-side down, onto the paper. Her handprint should be clearly outlined on the paper. Quickly, before she paints anything else, wash her hand. Now repeat the same procedure with our own hands. Put our handprints on the same sheet as Wanda's.

Invite Jack and Sue to add their handprints to the collection. This would be an excellent opportunity to affirm each family member's uniqueness by pointing out the differences among the prints. Let the children examine their handprints under the magnifying glass and explain that each person has his or her own handprint. Emphasize the swirls and wrinkles that make each one unique. Tell them that God created each child to be one of a kind. Express our love and appreciation for their uniqueness.

After we've finished the handiwork, tape it to the refrigerator door or tack it to the family bulletin board as a reminder of each person's value and worth.

Share a snack together. Invite Wanda to thank God for the snack and for her family. Ask each child to help plan another family time.

Case Study 19

Analyze the following plans the Brown family made for a Familytime especially for their elementary-age child. The Brown family has three children: Wanda, a 4-year-old; Jack, a 9-year-old; and Sue, 14.

- Have the nine guidelines been followed?
- What appear to be the strengths and weaknesses of this plan?

Familytime Plans

Supplies: Paper, crayons or felt-tip markers, a tape measure or ruler, bathroom scales, a family picture album, a camera and film, ingredients for a simple cake and frosting.

Activity: Explain that the purpose is to make a family portrait without drawing a picture. Instead, list important facts about family members.

Write each family member's name across the top of a large sheet of paper. Draw lines marking off a column for each person. Include the following information for each person: weight and height; shoe size; hair color and eye color; birthplace (city and state); talents and abilities; hobbies and special interests; favorite color, food, sport, game, book, vacation spot, music, Bible verse, Bible character, TV program, ice cream, animal, season, and holiday. Read the list together and talk about the way family members are alike and different.

Sit together so that everyone can see the family picture album. Look at the pictures together. Take time to remember and talk about special events such as births, parties, holidays, and vacations.

Looking at each child's first picture, say, "_______, you were a special baby because ... and now you are even more special to our family because. ..." Finish the sentence by mentioning a unique contribution that child makes to the family.

Take some new family pictures for the family album as family members prepare and eat the refreshments.

Display the family portrait of likes and differences on the refrigerator. Place the photographs in the family picture album, label them "Our Family Night," and date them. Have a prayer together; then plan the next family night.

Case Study 20

Analyze the following plans the Brown family made for a Familytime especially for their teenager. The Brown family has three children: Wanda, a 4-year-old; Jack, a 9-year-old; and Sue, 14.

- Have the nine guidelines been followed?
- What appear to be the strengths and weaknesses of this plan?

Familytime Plans

Supplies: Yarn or string, clothespins, three-by-five-inch cards or half sheets of typing paper, felt-tip markers, a family picture album, a camera and film, homemade pizza mix and toppings.

Activity: Explain that the purpose of this activity is to recognize and list the important events in the family's life. Begin with the date when the parents met and list important dates up to the present, such as weddings, birthdays, going to school, moving, new jobs, graduations, and so forth.

Keep in mind that family events may also represent illness, divorce, or death. Be prepared to discuss these events if the children seem concerned or ask questions.

When the list is made, make a family time line. String a line from one doorway to another or from one window to another. Write a short description of each event and its date on cards or half sheets of typing paper. Clip them on the line in chronological order.

When the time line is completed, ask these questions: What will be the next major events in our family? How do we feel about them? Are these coming events causes for worry or joyful anticipation or both?

Sit together so that everyone can see the family picture album. Look for pictures that illustrate the events in the family time line. Pick out some pictures that illustrate changes in the family, such as new babies, enlarging the family, children growing up, new houses, or new hobbies or jobs. As we look at pictures that show how much our children have grown and changed, say: "You have grown and changed so much over the past few years. I am proud of the way you are. ..." Finish the sentence by affirming something the child is doing that shows maturity.

Take some new family pictures for the family album as family members prepare and eat the refreshments. Invite Sue to thank God for the refreshments.

Session 10

Parents: Sharing and Supporting

Session Goals

After completing this session, members should better understand the importance and value of parents' sharing with and supporting one another. They will be able to

- state four benefits of a parent-support group;
- identify two unique problems single-parent and blended families sometimes encounter;
- name at least two periodicals that provide resource material for parent-support groups;
- commit to participate in a parent-support group for at least two months, meeting monthly.

Before the Session

1. Carefully study lesson 10 and complete all of the learning activities.
2. Duplicate worksheets 3 (to use as a posttest), 25, and 26 and case studies 21, 22, and 23.
3. Write the following statements on large sheets of newsprint. Mount the sheets in random order on the walls around the room.
   - Parents who meet together can find strength and support.
   - Parents have to discover their own ways.
   - Parents can try new ideas in a supportive atmosphere with other parents.
   - Parental influences are apparent in children's behavior.
   - Parents can learn about their own values by sharing with other parents.
   - A parent can say, "Help!" in a parent-support group.
   - Single-parent and blended families have unique challenges and opportunities.
   - Comparisons among children can destroy their sense of unique worth.
   - All parents should be consistent in enforcing rules.
   - Parenting requires a prayerful approach.
   - Parenting by grace works.
   - Parenting by grace is not a quick fix.
   - Parenting by grace is an attitude that comes from God's gift of grace.
4. Obtain enough copies of *ParentLife* and *Living with Teenagers* for each member to have a copy of the periodical related to his or her age child. Check in your church media library for books about family concerns. Bring as many as you can to the session. Arrange these resources on a table in the room.

During the Session

1. Welcome members. Ask for prayer requests and call on someone to lead in prayer.

DEBRIEFING

2. Review lesson 9. Ask members to share their experiences with Familytime during the past week.
3. Refer to lessons 1–9, using the outline poster. Distribute copies of worksheet 3 and ask members to complete the posttest. Have members compare their responses with the pretests they completed prior to session 1. Discuss any item about which anyone has a question. Answers: 1. T, 2. F, 3. F, 4. F, 5. F, 6. T, 7. T, 8. T, 9. T, 10. T, 11. F, 12. F, 13. T, 14. F, 15. F, 16. T, 17. T, 18. F, 19. F, 20. T, 21. T, 22. F, 23. F, 24. T, 25. F. Also ask these questions:
   - What have you enjoyed most about the course?
   - What is one important truth you believe God has taught you during this course?
   - What is one action you will resolve to take based on your study?

PRESENTATION

4. Refer to "Checkpoint" on page 94 in the *Parent's Guide.* Ask members to share their work.
5. Ask members to share in pairs their evaluations of the help they have received from the parent-support group in this course (p. 92 in the *Parent's Guide*).

SKILL DEVELOPMENT

6. With members still divided in pairs, assign the following role play. The objective is to illustrate the difference between lecturing to a child and having a discussion with a child.

   One person is the parent; the other is the child. First, role-play a situation in which the parent spoils a teachable moment by lecturing to the child. Use a typical question adolescents might ask, such as: Why don't I ever have any dates? What's wrong with me? Why won't you let me [have the car, go to the party, wear eye shadow, join the club]? or Why can you skip church on Sunday night, but I have to go?

Then ask members to switch roles and do another role play. The parent is confronted with the same question but discusses the answer with the child instead of lecturing.

After the role plays, discuss these questions:

- How did you feel in each situation, both as a parent and as a child?
- Which situation promoted more learning and a better feeling between parent and child? How?

Point out that a parent-support group permits parents to practice recommended principles of parenting.

7. Divide members into three or more small groups according to the ages of their children. If they have children in more than one age group, ask them to select one to which they would like to give attention. Assign case study 21 to parents of preschoolers, case study 22 to parents of elementary-age children, and case study 23 to parents of teenagers. Allow a few minutes for small-group work and then call for reports. Also use this activity to point out the value of discussing and practicing parenting guidelines with a parent-support group.
8. Distribute copies of worksheet 25. Ask members to discuss it in their small groups. Point out the value of sharing this type of activity in a parent-support group. Ask, What insights did you gain from other members as you discussed the activity?
9. Distribute copies of worksheet 26 and ask the small groups to discuss it. Point out that participation in a support group helps parents understand the significance of their behavior.
10. Encourage members of single-parent and blended families to share any unique problems or opportunities they experience. Relate how a support group can help in these situations.
11. Refer to the case study about Courtney on page 92 in the *Parent's Guide* and ask members how they responded.
12. Call attention to the table of resource materials. Ask members to examine the books and to select one they would be interested in studying. Distribute copies of *ParentLife* and *Living with Teenagers.* Note how these periodicals can help in the parenting process. After they examine the materials, allow an opportunity for any questions about or discussion of the resources.
13. Allow time for members to make plans for one or more parent-support groups. Do not take a strong lead in this activity but let members take the lead. Your job at this point is that of an encourager. This activity is the heart of this session, so allow sufficient time. Do not rush members as they make plans.
14. Call attention to the teaching poster "Parenting by grace is an attitude that comes from God's gift of grace." Use the material in "Conclusion" (p. 95 in the *Parent's Guide*) to challenge members to continue to parent by grace. Express appreciation to each member for completing the course.

ASSIGNMENT

15. Ask if any members need to make assignments or announcements about the parent-support group(s).

After the Session

1. Evaluate the session by referring to "After the Session" on page 26 in this guide.
2. Take time to evaluate the course thoroughly.
   - What would you do differently if you were leading the course again?
   - What growth have you experienced as a leader during the course?
   - Review the purpose of *Parenting by Grace: Discipline and Spiritual Growth* (see p. 5 in this guide). Do you believe the course's learning goal was achieved?
3. Complete Church Study Course credit requests for eligible participants.
4. Turn in attendance records to your Discipleship Training director.
5. When the *Parenting by Grace: Discipline and Spiritual Growth* Church Study Course Diplomas are received, present them to group members in a way that highlights the significance of their accomplishments:
   - In a church service
   - Individually with an announcement of their accomplishments printed in the newsletter
   - In a Sunday School or Discipleship Training department
   - At a special fellowship time with the group
   - In a combination of the above

WORKSHEET 25

Reflect on some of the everyday situations in your home. How are you handling them now? How can you handle them differently as you parent by grace? Complete the chart.

Situations with My Child	My Usual Responses	Parenting-by-Grace Responses

WORKSHEET 26

1. *The use of time.* On the chart below check the major activities you participated in last week, assuming that last week was a typical week. Circle each day when you spent at least 30 minutes with your child. Three activities are already listed. Write others.

	Sunday	Monday	Tuesday	Wednesday	Thursday	Friday	Saturday
Sleep							
Job							
Meals							

2. *The use of money.* Look at your checkbook register and charge-card statement for last month. Other than bare necessities, how did you spend your money?

____

____

____

3. From your use of time and money, what do you value most?

____

____

____

4. What changes should you make in how you spend your time and money?

____

____

____

Case Study 21

Analyze the following situation.

The bedtime ritual is finished—bath, pajamas, water, story, bathroom, prayers, and a good-night kiss. You tuck your four-year-old into bed and whisper: "I love you. Sleep well." You turn off the lights and walk slowly, quietly from the room.

Two minutes later you hear, "Mom, I can't sleep" or "Daddy, it's too dark in here." You make a trip to the bedroom. You give another kiss, another pat. Five minutes later, "Mom, I'm hot" or "Daddy, I see something in the corner." Again you go to the bedroom. For 10 or 15 minutes this scene is repeated. Then the crying starts. You get up from your chair and start toward the bedroom. ...

- What is your first reaction and the response you would like to make?
- How would that response make you feel?
- How would that response likely affect your preschooler?
- How could you respond with parenting by grace?

Case Study 22

Analyze the following situation.

Dad finds eight-year-old Peter struggling with a child in the neighborhood. The younger child has climbed over the backyard fence and has destroyed Peter's insect collection he was making for a school project. Dad sends Peter to his room. Fighting back tears, Peter flings himself across the bed facedown and refuses to talk.

- What is your first reaction and the response you would like to make?
- How would that response make you feel?
- How would that response likely affect your eight-year-old?
- How could you respond with parenting by grace?

Case Study 23

Analyze the following situation.

Joe is 16 and has his learner's permit to drive. He can legally drive if a licensed driver is in the seat beside him. When you get home from work, you discover that he drove the family's second car to school with a 16-year-old friend. You have already given clear instructions that he is not to drive unless you are with him.

- What is your first reaction and the response you would like to make?
- How would that response make you feel?
- How would that response likely affect your son?
- How could you respond with parenting by grace?

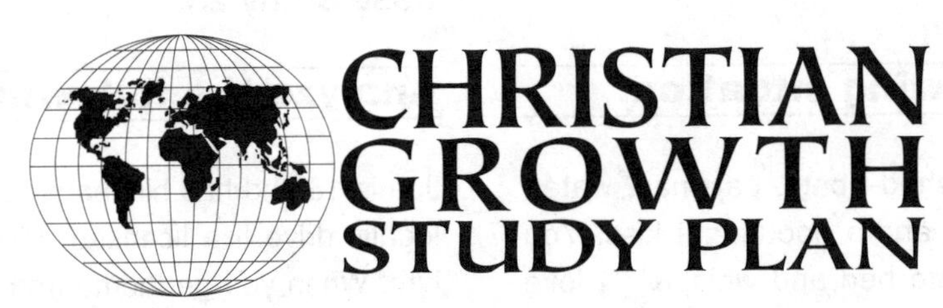

Preparing Christians to Serve

In the **Christian Growth Study Plan (formerly Church Study Course),** this book *Parenting by Grace: Discipline and Spiritual Growth* is a resource for course credit in the subject area Home/Family of the Christian Growth category of diploma plans. To receive credit, read the book, complete the learning activities, show your work to your pastor, a staff member or church leader, then complete the following information. This page may be duplicated. Send the completed page to:

Christian Growth Study Plan
127 Ninth Avenue, North, MSN 117
Nashville, TN 37234-0117
FAX: (615)251-5067

For information about the Christian Growth Study Plan, refer to the current Christian Growth Study Plan Catalog. Your church office may have a copy. If not, request a free copy from the Christian Growth Study Plan office (615/251-2525).

Parenting by Grace: Discipline and Spiritual Growth

COURSE NUMBER: CG-0209

PARTICIPANT INFORMATION

Social Security Number (USA ONLY)	Personal CGSP Number*	Date of Birth (MONTH, DAY, YEAR)
- -	- -	- -

Name (First, Middle, Last) ☐ Mr. ☐ Miss ☐ Mrs. ☐	Home Phone - -

Address (Street, Route, or P.O. Box)	City, State, or Province	Zip/Postal Code

CHURCH INFORMATION

Church Name		
Address (Street, Route, or P.O. Box)	City, State, or Province	Zip/Postal Code

CHANGE REQUEST ONLY

☐ Former Name		
☐ Former Address	City, State, or Province	Zip/Postal Code
☐ Former Church	City, State, or Province	Zip/Postal Code

Signature of Pastor, Conference Leader, or Other Church Leader	Date

*New participants are requested but not required to give SS# and date of birth. Existing participants, please give CGSP# when using SS# for the first time. Thereafter, only one ID# is required. **Mail to:** Christian Growth Study Plan, 127 Ninth Ave., North, Nashville, TN 37234-0117. Fax: (615)251-5067